BE A GRADUATE

*Ace your assignments
and exams without
burning out in
easy study formula.*

YOLANDA HIEW, PhD

Copyright © 2021 by Yolanda Hiew, PhD.

ISBN:	Hardcover	978-1-5437-6613-4
	Softcover	978-1-5437-6611-0
	eBook	978-1-5437-6612-7

All rights reserved. No part of this book may be used or reproduced by any means, graphic, electronic, or mechanical, including photocopying, recording, taping or by any information storage retrieval system without the written permission of the author except in the case of brief quotations embodied in critical articles and reviews.

Because of the dynamic nature of the Internet, any web addresses or links contained in this book may have changed since publication and may no longer be valid. The views expressed in this work are solely those of the author and do not necessarily reflect the views of the publisher, and the publisher hereby disclaims any responsibility for them.

Print information available on the last page.

To order additional copies of this book, contact
Toll Free +65 3165 7531 (Singapore)
Toll Free +60 3 3099 4412 (Malaysia)
orders.singapore@partridgepublishing.com

www.partridgepublishing.com/singapore

TABLE OF CONTENTS

Foreword vii
Preface xi
Acknowledgments xv
Introduction xvii

Chapter 1   Why College Students Drop Out 1
Chapter 2   What Is Your Goal 9
Chapter 3   What to Expect in College 20
Chapter 4   How to Start Your New Semester 31
Chapter 5   How to Manage Your Time 45
Chapter 6   How to Tackle Assignments 56
Chapter 7   How to Collaborate in Group Work 69
Chapter 8   How to Prepare for Final Exams 79
Chapter 9   How to Remember What You Learn 93
Chapter 10 How to Handle Relationships 101
Chapter 11 How to Live a Healthy Life 111
Chapter 12 What Is College Depression 124
Chapter 13 Where to Get More Help 136

Inspirational Success Stories 149
Bibliography 155
About the Author 159

FOREWORD

"The brain is like a parachute. It's only useful when it's open."

The reason why most smart students fail is they don't know how to study, so the brain shuts down when they try to study. Nothing gets retained, facts forgotten, blank during exams, and smart students fail!

That's the big difference between knowing *what* to study and *how* to study!

The question is, how to open up the brain?

Albert Einstein's famous quote "Curiosity is more important than knowledge" reveals the truth. Curiosity leads to interest that instigate attention and staying focused, which gives better retention and improved marks in exams.

That's my aspiration, to spark a deep curiosity for learning, and I can give myself a pat on the back if the learner who sits in my class walks out of the classroom with a curiosity to continue learning and becomes a lifelong learner!

It is my passion, over the last two decades, to inspire lifelong learning in every student. When I left my five-year teaching profession as a secondary school teacher to start my own education center in Singapore, I knew it was not going to be a typical learning center. Genius IQ was born out of that deep desire to help students learn how to study and offer emotional management tools for maximum success. Part of that holistic approach is to educate parents on positive parenting skills so they can also support the child in learning how to learn to improve their school grades and well-being.

Another signature program that I have been conducting is the Secrets to Exam Success that has helped over one hundred thousand primary and high school students internationally in the past twenty years for greater self-esteem and belief in their own potentials by upgrading their minds to think out of the box.

As the saying goes, "A good teacher provides knowledge and information, but a great teacher inspires learning!"

In this book, *Be a Graduate*, Dr. Yolanda Hiew truly inspires and empowers tertiary students to ultimately pass the exams and get a degree, which is every student's dream. She shares her story of achievements in her own educational journey and her mission to empower students' academic success holistically. I'm beyond thrilled as we share a similar vision on the true meaning of education!

The author is the epitome of an educator, given her shining credentials. She continues to unlearn and relearn and is the ambassador of a lifelong learner. Being an active student in my programs, she is one who walks the talk; first, transforming her profession through personal development to become a life coach and entrepreneur, and then as a parent, to enhance her skills in positive parenting.

This book is indeed a unique study skills guide for students' academic excellence. It is not simply a book for college students to score in exams, but also a life manual, a dire need in our changing and challenging times in the millennial generation; one that addresses education beyond just academics but as a synergistic interaction of study skills and the emphasis toward the mind, emotion, body, and health, as a tool to excel in higher learning, personal growth, and beyond.

As a nutritionist by profession, I believe nutrition plays an important role in the brain development and supporting the immune system of each child so they grow healthily. This book brilliantly presents a chapter that is essential for college students to learn how to live a healthy lifestyle with proper diet while studying.

From tackling assignment and exam preparation to time management and handling relationships, this book comes in handy for students who are burned out, depressed, and unable to focus on their studies. The author diligently includes a chapter that explains well on college students' depression and how parents and teachers can assist to prevent it.

While using herself as an example of a graduate in her book, Dr. Hiew covers all the elements of what is needed exactly for a college student in this era to survive and excel in study and in life. Clearly written, well organized, and enormously practical, this book should be in every college's and university's professional library, a must-read for those who aspire to do well and obtain a bachelor's degree qualification.

Suria Sparks
Celebrity Nutritionist
Founder of Genius IQ Positive Parenting

PREFACE

Your brain will work tirelessly to achieve the statements you give your subconscious mind. And when those statements are the affirmations and images of your goals, you are destined to achieve them!

—*Jack Canfield*

I aspire to help students become a graduate and high achiever in life without stress or burning out in the shortest time possible. I am sure you want a solution to your study problem that you are facing right now. I want to share with you how I completed my tertiary study successfully in every course, and I want to teach you how you can do the same by following my step-by-step guide. I am indebted to the study skills of best-selling author Stella Cottrell, whom I have learned from her *Success Skill Student Handbook* when I was studying at the University of East London in 1997 and I have attended her lecture. Stella's handbook has helped me in my study to the finishing line. I obtained a second upper class honors degree.

This book, *Be a Graduate*, is targeting freshmen or school-leavers, preuniversity and undergraduate students like you who may have difficulty in reading fast and taking notes during lecture and challenges such as getting your assignments done, working as part of a team, remembering what you learned, and relationship problems.

I was not a straight A or top student. I was an average student, but I know, with the right skills and determination to succeed, you can get through your study much easier. I have been studying, teaching, and learning all my life and have not stopped learning since I finished my formal schooling up to gaining a doctorate. My principle is that once I start a course, I would complete it in time no matter what happened. You can do it, too. I can help you to become better at studying, achieve higher grades in exams, and to be more confident in your life. The basic survival skills you learn in this book also help you build a habit in your lifelong learning for personal development after graduation. It is my duty to impart my knowledge to help you and many students to be successful in studies and in life. My wish for you is that you achieve your goal, get the degree you deserve, embrace your values, keep on learning, and live your dreams!

What triggered my interest in the content of this book is the high rates in students suicide statistics around the globe. Thus, depression and suicide are of increasing concern on college campuses, with one in four young adults aged eighteen to twenty-four diagnosed with mental illness. In a survey, 16 percent of college students reported being diagnosed with a depressive disorder, many within the last year. Over 90 percent of students who commit suicide have a diagnosable mental disorder. Research study shows during the 2019 to 2020 school year, over one-third of university and college students in the US screened positive for moderate to severe symptoms of depression.

Student suicide cases are on the rise worldwide, and it caught my attention few years ago. I heard the shocking news about a student who plunged to his death at his university campus when he didn't get the exam results he expected, and feeling too embarrassed to face his parents and peers. I was saddened by the news. A recent survey by Boston University reveals depression in young people now reaching its highest levels, a sign of the mounting stress factors due to the coronavirus pandemic. According to a survey at BestColleges.com, 95 percent of college students have experienced negative mental health symptoms as a result of COVID-19-related circumstances.

Many parents don't know what to do when their college-going children face the challenges of college depression, apart from other personal matters like relationship and money issues the students face. I wrote two e-books and published via an online platform to create awareness on student stress. My main purpose for the e-books was to eliminate further suicidal attempts, and I was hoping that more students, teachers, and parents would read and understand why college students drop out. I believe these students have a dream and are with high hopes, but they couldn't make it to the finishing line.

Thus, the main purpose of this book is to teach students how to survive in college and university, helping them to help themselves get through their studies. Learning about study skills for higher academic levels is crucial for you as a student, which gives you the opportunity to develop the personal skills that are transferable to employment after graduation. Students who dropped out of college are either a genius pursuing their dreams or lacking knowledge in their study and personal skills. Once you know the secret of how to study and cope with exams, you will get through all your struggles and become a graduate before you realize it! This book emphasizes not only the skills required to succeed in college, but also includes the importance of knowing what to expect in college, how to handle relationships, how to live a healthy life and to be mindful of matters that blend into a student's life, where most study skills books don't cover.

The ultimate aim of higher education is not getting straight As or a first-class degree, but learning how to learn and focusing on what you do at the present moment is a vital life skill here. I spent hours scouring study techniques books and research journals to find the best ways to learn more effectively. Hence the existence of this book. I'm a lifelong learner, and I have since completed my highest formal education. Over the course of my academic career, I have used most of the tips outlined in this book and taught them to my students, who have also benefited from the techniques. I can ensure that these learning techniques will work for you if you follow through! Have faith. Be thankful.

ACKNOWLEDGMENTS

I dedicate this book to the memory of my father, Stephen S. K. Hiew, who embraced hope, patience, and perseverance. His love of life, positive mindset, and generous spirit were a continuous source of inspiration to me. I'm thankful for his love, trust, and encouragement toward my academic success journey.

My deep appreciation for my beloved daughter, Jade, for being a huge part of my personal success.
A big thank-you to my wonderful family and friends who have encouraged me to write this book.

My gratitude to Lai Yong Yin, Patrick Hiew, and Asher Aw, who have shared their inspirational academic achievements. I believe that their contributions would greatly inspire many individuals who aspire to be a graduate.

I'm thanking God for His highest blessings for the publication of this book and that this book has been a calling to reach you in time.

INTRODUCTION

*The greatest achievement in life is to overcome the obstacles
and make your dreams come true, no matter what.*
—Dr. Yolanda Hiew

I taught my students how to study the right way and dream big. Little did I realize it helped them so much in scoring their exams and finally got what they wanted. They graduated! I would like to tell you how I came to be a university professor after being rejected from a teacher's training college, and how this book came into existence.

At the age of seven, I set my ambition to become an English teacher. I just love teaching. I played with my dolls and teddy bears, sat them on the couch, and started imagining that they were my little pupils and I would teach them something. If they were naughty, I would scold and show them how to read and write, using my imagination, just like how my schoolteacher did. I'm the youngest in the family, and all my other siblings are much older than me, so I'm usually very alone at home playing and talking by myself. Throughout my childhood, I always imagined what I wanted to be, have, and do. Nobody taught me about what imagination can do for my future. I daydreamed a lot—to live in a better place, have better things, be with better people. Each time I watched a movie, from the words spoken and scenes played, I got carried away and fantasized how I could become that person, have what they have, and do what they do. Then I acted on it, pretending to be that person, speaking like her, and driving the car she drives—in my imagination!

Sounds crazy, right?

At twelve, I became popular in school. I dared to challenge the teachers at times. I was an introvert, but I was not timid. I have a few good friends who I am still in contact with to this day. I was also curious about life. *Why am I in this world?* I grew up in a Catholic family but was not an active churchgoer. Every year, my mother would get me to attend midnight mass with her on Christmas Eve, Good Friday, and Easter. It's a tradition to have a Christmas cake at home, and that's really a luxury. We didn't exchange Christmas presents, and that could be the reason I'm not fond of Christmas gifts, as I don't remember when was the first time I received a present for Christmas. I have learned in school that Santa Claus would give presents and chocolates to children, but I had never seen a real Santa Claus before. I was curious about what Santa Claus has got to do with Christmas. As a kid who loved school and trying to make friends, I hung out with some teenage girls in my neighborhood, and most of them were into everything except their studies. They loved talking about boys, and I was too shy to join them as I was not into boys. I liked their company though, and we did nice craftwork, which I learned a lot from them. They enjoyed the outdoors, and they said studying is boring and homework sucks. Not long after, they started dating; each had her own boyfriend, and so we lost touch.

As a teenager, I wanted to do what other teenagers did, and so I had to break my shyness of being an introvert. Boys were all over me due to my looks. So I also became popular in secondary school. My mother always reminded me not to date any boy because I had to study so that I could get a good job with a decent pay. I wanted to become a teacher, but my mother said, "Don't ever work as a teacher because you won't get good pay." I listened to her, but I was not happy. Teaching is a respectful, caring profession. Is it really about money when it comes to one's passion? What did the outside world look like? I just had to go out there and see it myself, and I was mature enough to take care of myself. This time I became quite rebellious because I wanted freedom. I may have looked like an extrovert, but deep down, I was vulnerable and upset about the restrictions placed on me, like going to parties with my friends.

I was thirteen, and most of my friends were my seniors; they were sixteen and above, but my mature look was a disguise. I looked more mature and taller than my party friends, so they sneaked me to a disco bar. All of them, boys and girls, had no interest in studying for their future; they were partying even days before their exams.

My father used to work far away from home and came back two or three times a year and stayed for a week the longest. As a partygoer, I often hung out with the girls, and became like them, secretly drinking and smoking. I didn't like to study anymore. I loved the freedom of having any friends I chose and doing what I liked. I felt a sense of belonging, and I enjoyed their company. At one point, I thought of running away from home as nobody really cared, but I had nowhere to go. One night after a crazy night out with the girls, I came home past midnight and saw my father waiting in the living room. My mother might have told him that I misbehaved as I was no longer listening to her, being so-called rebellious at times. I was so surprised because my father had never been so serious with me or any of my siblings. He was a friendly, patient, and generous person who never scolded anyone, and I rarely saw his frustration, unlike my mother. It was this one thing that he said to me that has made me come to my realization of what I was doing and how much my parents put their hope on me. Being the youngest in the family and the only child who studied in a Chinese school, it served my father well because he was Chinese educated. I thought he didn't care about my studies since he was not home most of the time; not only that he never asked anything about my studies, he didn't watch me grow up too.

That night changed my life forever!

My father said, "Your priority now is to focus on your studies, and partying won't guarantee a bright future. With a good education, you stand a better chance in everything you do." That's all. After those two sentences, he went to bed. I cried, feeling confused, regretful, and so much guilt; and there were so many things running through my head, and I stayed awake that night. Suddenly, I remembered my dreams—to be an English teacher when I grow up, a dream I had when I was seven. I wanted to achieve my dreams and be highly educated. I was only thirteen, and from there, I found my big why. I was hoping that my parents would be proud of me someday. Unfortunately, I failed in my final grading in the Chinese independent school. I got 59 percent, and the passing score was 60 percent. I appealed but wasn't successful. I didn't want to retain another year in the same school, so my mother helped me with the transfer to a girls' school where it's a Malay medium school. I had a hard time studying because of the transition from a bilingual English-and-Chinese school to a school with all the core subjects in Malay language.

The first year of the transition had been tough, and I was always laughed at by one teacher while despised by another because I couldn't answer the questions in their lessons. However, I slowly caught up in the first year, and the following year, I passed all the subjects. I worked twice as much or harder than my friends and was promoted to the best art stream. I asked my mother for private tuition to improve my two weakest subjects to prepare for my national exams. I knew what I wanted. I had been daydreaming about my future, imagining what I would achieve in the future, every night before bed and the first thing in the morning. I visualized my graduation day, where I would be wearing a gown and a mortarboard, receiving my scroll on stage, and I could hear the crowd cheering for me, and I felt the excitement. That vision kept playing on my mind for years, even after leaving school.

The day came when I received my high school national exam results, and immediately I applied to study education and English at a local teacher's training college. I was so devastated that my application was rejected, and it crushed my longtime ambition to become a teacher because now I couldn't get into a college that would serve my passion with a possible bright future. What was I going to do at eighteen? I didn't have a plan B. I kept dreaming and visualizing what I wanted to be. I dared not think of how to do it as I really didn't know how. So I started finding a job and landed in a tuition center to teach English. Yes, my first job was as an English tutor. Due to ridiculously low pay that wasn't even sufficient for me to cover my daily lunch, I left to seek a higher-pay position. In five years, I had tried six to seven different jobs while studying short courses part-time at a local college. In between, I applied to become an air stewardess and was rejected twice from two different airlines due to my poor eyesight. Again, I was devastated because I couldn't afford to study full-time unless I saved enough money with a better-paying job, and the cabin crew opportunity was one good option. I was not eligible for any scholarship or a bank loan. My family obviously was not able to send me for further education. My parents were retired. But I didn't want to give up on my dreams. I prayed. I visualized.

Then after all the banking, accounts and admin jobs, I finally joined a Japanese school, and I enjoyed teaching English at the school that was attended by purely Japanese students of expats and teachers from Japan. While teaching there, my boyfriend got a scholarship to study in England, so he left to pursue his dreams. We were in a distant relationship for some time, and occasionally he would call me, apart from writing letters to each other. That was the time, I remember, we really missed each other. He encouraged me to study too, so he found a way for me to join him in England. I had never left my hometown before, and England is thousands of miles away from Malaysia. My parents were so worried that I'd be far away with no money, and how was I going to survive! But I was desperate for an opportunity and considering my prayers were answered. I promised my parents I would come back as a graduate with an honors degree. I didn't know how I would achieve that, but that's what I promised them. I flew to London and landed with three part-time jobs and a course to study in a foreign place far from home, with a big goal to get a higher education degree.

So I did. I was so fortunate I learned study skills at the university. It made studying a lot easier. I graduated with an honors bachelor degree in education and major in linguistics. Two years later, I got my master's degree in applied linguistics, sponsored by a scholarship award I obtained from the university. My boyfriend and I were married, and we worked hard and supported each other. I was going to study for my doctorate degree, but we decided to start a family as my age was catching up, and he was studying a second degree with one more year to complete. So we agreed that I would pursue my doctorate after having a baby. A year before, my husband was diagnosed with a heart disease, and he had been on medication. Eight months after our daughter was born, he passed away in his sleep due to heart failure.

We attended my husband's graduation just one month before his passing, and he had fulfilled his goals to complete his studies. I broke down in disbelief, crying sick but without tears. I looked at my baby girl, and I didn't know what the future held for us. After a decade in England, we pursued and achieved our dreams. It was supposed to be a lovely family we had started. Now my little girl had lost her father. Never would I have expected such a life could strike me all of a sudden, right before my eyes, when everything seemed so perfectly planned for us.

I returned to Malaysia with my daughter as I didn't think I could cope with the loss. I needed moral and emotional support from my family. As a widow, I had mourned for a long time. Later on, I came across Buddhism and practiced the dharma for more than ten years. It has helped me tremendously healing my mind and soul. With my higher educational background, it has made it easier for me to grasp and follow the Buddhist teachings. I grew up in a Catholic family, but I was too shallow with the Bible, and I couldn't comprehend the gospel. When I became more educated in Buddhism and meditation and gained wisdom through the dharma, which has been an eye-opening experience, it led me into understanding the Bible and gospel better and the whole purpose of Christianity. I believe God has His plan for me throughout my life journey.

My late husband and I had only one mission—to study as much as we could in higher education and educate our children well. We never gave up, despite my husband being ill while studying at the university; his persistence inspired me. He insisted that our daughter must finish her higher education, and that would fulfil our responsibility as parents. I had a hard time in the first year after returning to Malaysia, and my parents helped me look after my daughter while I went to work. I fulfilled not only my dreams but also my promises to my mother and father—now that I was a graduate. Because I have a university degree, I got a teaching position within a month of job hunting.

If anyone ever tells you that getting a degree is useless, don't believe them! Share with them what my father told me! Whether you will work according to what you studied, it doesn't matter. Stephen Spielberg, a filmmaker who has won three Oscars and numerous other awards, fulfilled his longtime dream when he went back to college and graduated at the age of fifty-six. The college dropout Stephen said that his bachelor's degree is the one he really wanted, as a thank-you to his parents. Higher education is status, and knowledge is power. Gaining a bachelor's degree was not the end of my academic success, as I also obtained the doctorate degree I dreamed of. From being rejected to study for a teacher's diploma to the acceptance for a doctorate degree and from a schoolteacher to a college lecturer to a university professor—it has all been a process in the journey of a seven-year-old dreamer. To me, it's a great achievement. Never give up on your dreams.

Sadly my father passed away just a month before my PhD convocation ceremony. I was hoping that he would see me on stage and be proud of me. This is how I interpret what my father told me that night: "When you are educated, you can do whatever you wish that can help you and others." Hence the existence of this book. I came this far, and my little eight-month-old girl born in London is now eighteen. I'm grateful and thankful for this lifetime of what God has planned and crafted for me.

This book represents the essence of my study and teaching experience, as far as it can be conveyed in words, with my former colleagues and students during the past twenty years in England and Malaysia. This book is also, through my research, combined with the latest learning skills that are incorporated with technology and virtual classes. Every chapter is essential to read, and take action as soon as the semester starts. Take this book as your guide and see it as a personal coach to help you in your studies. Don't just read it once, refer to it again and again.

I am exceptionally obsessed with new knowledge and skills. My passion for teaching and helping others score higher have also led to a passion for lifelong learning. I enjoy sharing my experiences and knowledge with people, especially college students of any cultural background. I used to teach immigrants English for communication in an adult college in England, a great country where I lived for more than a decade. Since completing my PhD, I am still learning new things and using the skills I acquired into my new horizons. I am also guiding my daughter, who's going to college soon for her foundation year, using the content I wrote in this book. What I'm giving you here is exactly what I give my daughter for her success journey in higher education—a promise that my late husband and I have for our daughter. My main purpose here is to inspire you to get into college, learn how to study the easy way, and be a graduate. Therefore, this book reveals my secret formula to help in your study journey.

The Study-Made-Easy Formula

Over the years, as a student, I have gone through trial and error in learning how to study and the way to pass exams and be above average in coursework marks. Then, as a teacher, both in tertiary and high school, I tried my best to educate my students and help solve their study challenges, teaching them essential skills like English, positive thinking and study skills. I believe that having to master only study skills alone is not enough and won't get you to the finishing line easily, unless you also look into your mindset and body that is positive and healthy in order to achieve your goals. Thus, the success formula I created and applied is as follow:

Study Skills + Positive Mindset + Optimum Health = A Happy Graduate

The chapters of this book make up the formula and each is interrelated for your success as a student and beyond. Visit my website at **www.dryolandahiew.com** to learn more about self-motivation and positive mindset.

My wish for you is that you take the first step to learning the important skills today, get a degree, and ultimately achieve your dreams and lifelong ambition.

CHAPTER 1

WHY COLLEGE STUDENTS DROP OUT

Action is the foundational key to all success.
—Pablo Picasso

Why do some college students not make it to the finishing line? Throughout my international and multicultural teaching experiences at various institutions for more than twenty years, I have seen and spoken to thousands of students who played truant, missed lessons, came late for classes, had family problems, worked part-time, and so on. Being a teacher and advisor, I have heard all sorts of reasons given to me when I asked the students about their problems and why they were absent from class.

I began to take note and did an observation on whether students who performed poorly at tertiary level actually related to personal issues or the environment that has failed them. I compiled my findings about the mistakes these tertiary students made and discovered that the challenges were mainly due to lacking knowledge in study skills and that they had no idea how to seek help to survive at college. I have listed ten common reasons college students fail and drop out in their first year.

College students who perform poorly or fail during their first year make similar types of mistakes. What are these mistakes, and how are we to overcome them?

Mistake 1: Students lack self-motivation and are unwilling to commit themselves to self-improvement. They want to be spoon-fed and are unable to handle independence. (See chapters 2 and 4.)

Mistake 2: Those who fail actually lack the will to persist because they have little or no career interest. They have no knowledge of employers' demands. The parents want them to study a course they don't like. Consequently, they do not have any idea of why they are in college. (See chapters 2 and 3.)

Mistake 3: Less time spent studying, more on procrastination and other factors that take students away from their studies far too often (e.g., job, social media, games, friends, and family matters). (See chapters 5 and 10.)

Mistake 4: Students get disoriented at college and do not know how to seek help, such as educational and study issues, English language, financial assistance, skill workshops, and personal support available to them on campus. (See chapter 13.)

Mistake 5: Priorities of students include parties, dating, clubbing, outdoor activities, employment, social media, college clubs, and social friends, which do not include study schedules for educational progress. (See chapters 2 and 5.)

Mistake 6: Not having a clear idea of what college life is like or how to study effectively. They are afraid of exams, overwhelmed with the memorization and the amount of work required. (See chapters 3 and 9.)

Mistake 7: Students have a negative attitude about themselves, their friends, their tutors, their classes, their college, their neighborhood; they then begin to have poor health and are overstressed. They often verbally express this attitude but deny their depression. (See chapters 11 and 12.)

Mistake 8: Students are influenced by the environment (shopping, online games) and surrounded by high school friends who are not goal achievers and not interested in pursuing their studies, family who are unsupportive, and boy-girl relationships. (See chapters 2 and 10.)

Mistake 9: Poor performers miss classes or attend lectures infrequently or as they like or based on mood. They rely on others for their assignments, never turn up for group work meetings, never prepare for exams, and have no idea how to take lecture notes. (See chapters 3, 6, 7, and 8.)

Mistake 10: Students have chosen the wrong course. Poor grades on exams and coursework discourage students from reviving their studies. They simply give up, not knowing how to deal with study challenges and feeling hopeless. (See chapters 6 and 8.)

Through my observation on students of different cultural backgrounds studying at the tertiary level, I also discovered that college dropouts are not poor in their intelligence. In fact, they are simply weak in learning how to learn and how to get help to solve their problems. These students do not usually want to approach the advisor or student counselor on campus due to personality reasons. For example, the timid ones are too shy while the aggressive ones are too proud or embarrassed to talk about their studies and personal problems.

Students at higher education institutions face many kinds of challenges that negatively affect their psychological feelings, causing them anxiety. A recent study found that the most important factor that causes anxiety is related to academic study (Alkandari 2020). For example, many students who study a new language such as English face challenges in understanding language words, speaking, and writing. This issue was found in many students in different countries such as Korea, Thailand, Indonesia, China, and Saudi Arabia, which reflect that such an issue is widespread internationally among higher education institutions. Its effects vary among students in how to deal with the issue, overcome its symptoms, and find solutions. Here are some of the basic facts you need to know as a college student.

The Transition

Going from high school to college is a big transition. Give yourself time to adjust. Make new friends on campus by joining clubs or organizations that line up with your interests and values. Having a strong support system can help you feel better. You may even create a little study group with peers in your course program so that you can not only work on assignments and prepare for exams together, but also share your unique experiences in the subject. A sense of community and belonging is imperative to success in college.

Choose the Right Course

University is a great place to learn about yourself, and if a student discovers that they are studying the wrong degree, it can lead to them dropping out. How to avoid choosing the wrong course? When deciding what you want to study, you should spend time seriously thinking about it and trying to understand what you enjoy and will be happy doing every day. Avoid following the pack or picking a degree for the sake of the following: lower fees, popularity, your friend has chosen it, it's demanded by employers, and because your parents say so. Make sure to look into what you are passionate about and interested in, and decide what to study according to your desire. At the end of the day, it is your responsibility toward your chosen course and destiny.

Additionally, if you are unhappy with your course and want to avoid dropping out, you can often change your degree program, especially in the first year. Speak to the admin department in your faculty or student advisors at your college or university to see what you need to do to change your course. That way you can avoid dropping out and get to study what you truly are passionate about.

Money Matters

Before you start college, you need to have a solid financial plan that can make college more affordable. You may be wondering, "What can I do now to afford my future college tuition?" As a high school–leaver, you can start applying for scholarships and grants and other types of financial aid. Scholarships and grants differ from loans in that they do not have to be repaid. Additionally, you can look into work-study options, where you essentially pick up a part-time job on campus and have your salary go directly toward your college tuition expenses.

Bear in mind that some institutions may offer more financial aid than others. If your dream institution doesn't offer enough financial aid to cover tuition, don't be discouraged. Consider taking a year off to work and save up money, or enroll in a community college for two years and then transfer to the university of your choice. Community colleges are a lot cheaper than courses in colleges and universities, so you'll be able to save a good chunk of cash this way. If your parents can afford to pay for your tuition fees until you graduate, then you will have every reason to excel in your studies.

Curbing Stress

Trying to take too many classes at once while juggling a job and a healthy social and personal life can be tough, especially for freshmen. That being said, it's a good idea to take a step back and see where you can mitigate stress. For example, reading motivational books or watching inspirational videos for twenty minutes a day can play the trick for the first two semesters that may allow you to get the hang of college life. Though stress is normal and part of a student's life, it can be harmful if you don't manage it in a healthy manner.

Set a Schedule

It's important to set boundaries for yourself so that you can have fun responsibly without "losing it." Remember that balance is key! Setting a schedule is a great place to start. It will give you a sense of structure to each day, and you will be more likely to not only get your coursework taken care of, but also remember to eat during mealtimes, go to the gym regularly, and make it to class on time. Set a routine. Sometimes life in college can get hectic, so having—even if it's rough—a schedule to follow can make a big difference!

Having an accountability partner can also go a long way in boosting productivity if you are the type to lose motivation, if you are the only one holding yourself accountable. If this sounds like you, consider asking a coursemate or roommate to be your accountability buddy.

Get Help

Don't forget that your tutor, advisor, guidance counselor, and university professor are always at your disposal should you need assistance. Guidance counselors may help you get a clearer picture of what you want to major in if you are still on the fence, while lecturers or university professors hold office hours, providing the opportunity for students to drop in and get clarification one-on-one about a class topic. When I was a lecturer, course leader, and also a student advisor, I always hoped to see students come and see me with the challenges they face, because the sooner they solve it, the better. Unfortunately, they rarely appear.

Before you decide to drop out, consider talking to your professors, lecturers, and college counselors. Many times, they are willing to help you find a solution so that you can take some time off, such as deferring your study without sacrificing all your hard work and academic progress.

The following chapters present the skills you need to learn, master, and apply in order to be successful at higher education.

CHAPTER 2

WHAT IS YOUR GOAL

> Without goals, and plans to reach them, you are like a ship that has set sail with no destination.
> —Fitzhugh Dodson

If you want to achieve something, you need to have a *goal*. Goals are motivated by your dreams, desires, and plans, powered by discipline through commitment. Successful students regularly set achievable goals in their university studies. A goal without a deadline is just a wish. You need to make realistic plans to reach your goals; at the same time, you may expect issues to get in the way of your personal and academic progress. During the process of your studies, you may encounter the following:

- Procrastination
- Anxiety
- Self-doubt
- Depression
- Poor health
- Relationship problems
- Financial issues
- Low motivation
- Moodiness

Setting goals and attempting to achieve them is crucial for college students; it teaches them so much about themselves, about the world, and about life. But what are personal goal examples for students to get a better idea of how the goal-setting process works?

When I was a college student, I used to make long-term academic goals. In a small red diary, I drew a pyramid with four stages. The lowest base of the pyramid started with my college certificate/diploma, then a bachelor's degree, then a master's degree, and finally a doctorate at the tip of the pyramid. I achieved all of them! For my personal life, I set a goal to have a baby before the age of thirty-five. I had my daughter at thirty-three. I set a goal to get my doctorate before age forty-five, and I completed my PhD a year later, a bit overdue, and we have to accept that life is so unpredictable, and we just have to expect that the journey to every successful story has its rough path and hiccups.

This chapter will help you set your goals and achieve them in your academics, personal growth, money matters, and other areas of your life.

Dreams and Personal Goals

You may have a bigger dream, and you can break it down into smaller goals with a deadline to achieve them. For instance, my dream was to become a graduate with a degree from overseas. My first choice was England. I didn't have the money, and definitely my parents couldn't afford to send me to study in England. At age eighteen, it was my responsibility to decide what I wanted to do for my future. I made a decision, I focused on that decision, and I took action to imagine and visualize that I was already living in England. I imagined the cold weather, icy roads, and the university. Every night before I slept, I imagined myself wearing that gown and mortarboard, proudly receiving my scroll on stage on my graduation day. I had a good feeling with excitement, like it was real. Then the next morning, I imagined myself waking up in England. I didn't know how I would get there, but I knew that was my biggest dream, and I set some goals.

One of my goals was to apply for a course locally to qualify me to study in England. In fact, I applied for teachers training college after completing high school but was rejected, so I started my first job as a tutor in a local tuition center. Pay was so low I barely had enough for my daily lunch. I aimed for higher pay, so I kept switching jobs so that I could pay for my part-time study, mostly for jobs that allowed me to work during the day and attend evening classes. Another goal was to learn computer skills and study English to prepare for college or university entrance requirements. Then I checked out more information on universities in the UK from my local library and overseas agencies. I also tried to apply for scholarships and study loans, and all were unsuccessful. I wanted to study education, and I hadn't a clue how. I prayed a lot. I believed in myself. It's done. Opportunity came, and I grabbed it as I was ever ready. My dream came true exactly how I imagined it to be. A week before my twenty-fourth birthday, I arrived in London.

Dreams do come true. Goals are achievable. All you need to do is believe 100 percent that it will come true. Pray. Being thankful before you receive is called faith.

Academic Goals

As a college student, it is important to set academic goals as your priority. Many students tend to make goals for a new semester related to getting healthy, losing weight, spending more time with loved ones, saving more money, and so on. However, the most important goal for a college student is passing exams and moving to the next semester.

Exams tend to make up a big part of students' grades in college, so having good study habits is essential. Here are twelve study habits college students should make as their goals in the new semester.

1. Stop Procrastinating

When you put off studying until the last minute, you force yourself to cram for a test, and you are less likely to retain the information this way. Start scheduling study time further in advance before an exam so you don't have to spend hours and hours the few days before or the night before trying to review all the materials.

This may be a tough goal to have, but the more time you're able to spend with the information, the more likely you are to remember it and remember it correctly.

2. Never Skip Class

Going to class, taking notes, and starting to absorb and become familiar with the material, there is a key step that will help facilitate better studying. If you skip classes a lot, you will be forced to teach yourself the information and learn on your own, which means, when you could be reviewing your notes and studying, you will only be learning the material for the first time.

Make it your goal to actually go to all lecture classes this semester; you will have more and better information to study from if you attend class, and rereading what you wrote during class is a great and simple way to start your exam revision early.

3. Read Consistently

Along with attending classes, actually doing the assigned reading for your class is an important studying goal to have for this semester. When you do the assigned readings when they are supposed to be read, you allow yourself time to adequately read the textbook and other materials, and you'll be more prepared for your classes, which means more of the information lectured about and discussed in class will make sense speedily.

When you skim the readings or blow them off, you force yourself to cram, doing all the assigned readings into a day or two before the exam, when your time would be better spent simply reviewing your materials and notes, rather than completing other tasks you should have already done.

4. Review Notes

Don't just start reviewing and studying for a test a few days or the day before your exam. Instead, try to set aside time each day to review your notes. When you do go to study for a test, your retention rate will be much higher since you'll have already gone over the material multiple times and will remember the information better.

Resolve to review your notes for even just ten minutes each night so you become increasingly familiar with the material and much less stressed-out before the exam.

5. Choose a Study Spot

A good study spot is a crucial studying tool—so make it your goal to explore what locale will help you study productively. Many students find successful studying occurs in a campus library, but if you're more comfortable sticking to your dorm, apartment, or house, those places can work too.

Figure out what environment will allow you to concentrate the best, and try to schedule in some time to go there and study. Once you've found a good study spot, you may want to stick to it for all your studying.

6. Get Enough Sleep

Avoid burning the midnight oil. Rather than staying up super late cramming for an exam, make a goal to plan your studying schedule ahead so you can still get six to eight hours of sleep the night before your test. Being well-rested and getting enough sleep allows the information you studied to sink in, which will enable you to perform better on your tests.

7. Create a Study Routine

Habits are so powerful that once you develop a study routine, you will find it difficult to go into relaxation mode without studying. How should you go about creating a study routine? The first thing to do is to set up a study schedule.

Be aware, however, that habits are not formed overnight. Research indicates that it typically takes at least twenty-one days to form a new habit. So you will have to put in some work before this technique pays off. You can divide your tasks into smaller chunks. For example, when you are writing an essay, set a goal to finish the introduction. Try to write one section at a time. Once the introduction is completed, take a break, then continue the first body paragraph, and so on.

8. Aim for Good Grades

One of the best ways to get motivated to study is knowing why you want to obtain good grades. Make a list of your goals for things that you want to achieve academically. Here are some typical goals:

- I want to develop my study skills by the end of this semester
- I want to develop the habit of productivity at the start of the semester
- I want to be more focused in every lecture
- I want to score distinction for all my assignments
- I want to review all my lecture notes daily
- I want to read all materials in the reading list before doing assignments
- I want to learn academic writing this semester
- I want to improve on my communication in class this year
- I want to manage my time
- I want to stay resilient
- I want to think positive
- I want to attend every class

Write down your own list of goals for studying smart, and put the list at your study desk. Then when you're feeling unmotivated, read the list one more time. Also, set a goal to read a motivational book every month. Another way might be reading three pages of your textbook, completing three past year questions, or finding three journal articles on the Internet for your assignment.

9. Visualize Your Goals

If you're having trouble with a particular task, visualize yourself completing that task successfully. Sports psychologists have long known about the power of visualization as a technique for accomplishing difficult tasks. Visualization uses the "theater of the mind" to mentally rehearse completing challenging tasks. It works by laying down neural pathways in the brain.

When you repeatedly visualize yourself completing a task, it makes it easier to perform the task in reality. So spend a few minutes every day visualizing yourself successfully completing your various study-related tasks, especially if you find them daunting.

10. Reward Your Effort

Every time you complete one or two small tasks, reward yourself with a short period of relaxation. It could be five minutes on your smartphone, a short walk, or playing music. Rewarding yourself with short and enjoyable breaks is a key part of the "chunking down" technique. Learning the skills for success, and achieving your goals will boost your confidence as a student and will encourage you to keep on achieving.

11. Make SMART Goals

S – specific. Don't say, "I want to get a good result." Say, "I want to score an A for English." Pick a goal—a real goal. Something with specific reasons, requirements, and constraints. Specify a benefit.

M – measurable. Be able to measure your performance. A goal like "I want to write a five hundred–word essay in under thirty minutes" is great; you will know exactly when you've achieved it, and you have something to work toward. Something visible.

A – attainable. Make your goal something you can attain in the near future. If you can't even obtain sixty marks right now, don't make it your goal to achieve ninety marks right away. Shoot for seventy marks, make it, and then raise the bar.

R – relevant. Is this goal relevant to your life? It needs to really matter. A goal that does not really matter to your life's path isn't going to be fulfilled because you will not be able to keep yourself motivated. Say, "I want a grade A for English so that I can teach the language when I graduate."

T – time-bound. You need to set a time boundary for when this goal will be accomplished so you are motivated to practice because deadlines drive our performance. Write a deadline next to each goal.

12. Make a Vision Board

Example of Vision Board

A vision board needs to include anything that inspires you of which you want to achieve as a goal. It is a visualization tool that uses a board of any sort to build a collage of words and pictures that represents your goals and dreams. The best way to achieve your goals is to keep them top of mind so you are always looking for ways to move yourself closer to them, and a vision board is the perfect tool to help you do that.

Here's how you create a vision board for both your study and personal goals:

1. Make a list of important goals you want to achieve.
2. Collect a bundle of old magazines with colorful pictures or print the pictures online.
3. Find pictures that represent your goals and inspire you.
4. Make a collage out of those pictures, and write some words next to the picture.

Hang your vision board in front of your study desk or a place where you can see it every day. Take a photo of your vision board, and use it as your wallpaper on your smartphone and screensaver on your computer. You will prompt yourself to visualize your ideal life on a regular basis.

Set your goals, give each goal a deadline, and accomplish it. By making these twelve goals, your studies and life as a student will be more effective, and your exam scores will be better. However, these goals only work if you believe in them, review them, and take action! You don't have to share your goals or the vision board with anyone. Keep it to yourself. When you show success, your friends will ask how you did it. Then you show them this book and share your journey.

May you achieve all your goals.

CHAPTER 3

WHAT TO EXPECT IN COLLEGE

> The true sign of intelligence is not knowledge but imagination.
> —Albert Einstein

As a tertiary student, you are fully responsible for your own learning. In other words, your success depends on the effort you put into your journey of study. If your grades are not what you expected, it is not the fault of the lecturers or tutors, and do not blame fate, your parents, friends, any circumstances, or anybody. You have to make a commitment right now to become an independent, skilled, self-motivated, and disciplined learner. You will not be spoon-fed at college!

When I started my first semester at the University of East London (UEL) many years ago, I did not know what to expect. However, I was determined, excited, and prepared to start my journey as a university student. Throughout my three years as an undergraduate, I encountered racial discriminations from one or two of the lecturers and tons of stressful moments for assignments and exams. That did not affect me because my purpose at UEL was to get a degree. That's my dream. I did not have problems in English language and communication. My challenges were that I did not know how to take proper lecture notes because some lecturers talked really fast and in different accents. I also had no idea how to work as part of a team effectively or how to write academic essays since I was not taught about this in school. I had to learn the hard way.

Fortunately, I found several handbooks on tertiary study skills from the university library and read all of them to help me get through my study. One handbook written by Stella Cottrell had tremendously helped in many areas of my studies. So the first semester was quite a struggle for me, though I enjoyed the learning experience and never missed a class. With my step-by-step guide, you don't have to go through the difficult part and spend too much time reading piles of study skills books like I did. I am here to guide you through your study in a practical way based on my experience both as a learner and teacher. I want you to study smarter, not harder!

You can achieve greater success when you know what to expect in college. Thus, it is essential to attend the orientation to find out the names of your lecturers and the room or venue of all your classes. When the semester starts, expect to find that the number of students in a class or lecture hall varies according to the course. A tutorial class may have about ten to twenty-five students, while a lecture usually has anywhere from fifteen to eighty or more students.

Studying in college and university, you are expected to understand and remember what you read and learn from the lectures. You must keep up with your reading lists and complete your assignments as planned. You will also need critical thinking skills to form opinions, draw conclusions, and evaluate the ideas of others.

Upon knowing what to expect in college, here are five steps to help you build a successful trait in your first semester.

Step 1 - Be Present in Every Lecture

It is important to attend every class and tutorial. When you miss classes, you miss lectures, notes, class discussions, assignment explanations, and other information. You may also miss in-class quizzes and even tests.

Never think that missing one class has no difference in your study. It can be tempting to cut a class now because you don't have the mood to study or feel lazy, but this can lead to a bad habit to skip classes in the future whenever you like. The only time you don't go to class is when you are ill or there's a special event you can't avoid. Not when you are in a bad mood. In this case, you will have to get the notes from your coursemates, and it's usually more of a hassle as it's not a fair thing to do.

Despite the hassle, do make sure that you have a phone number or email address of at least one person in each class. If you are absent, you will have someone you can contact to find out what you missed. Getting the contact numbers and email addresses of your lecturers are also helpful when you have a question about an assignment or an upcoming test. Write a journal regularly to reflect on your learning and any challenges you may have.

Step 2 - Be Organized

Use a notebook, planner, or diary for your assignments. Take your assignment notebook to every class, and record each assignment. Break down the assignment into stages to accomplish each task.

For example, you receive the assignment on September 15, and the deadline for submission is September 30, set a deadline for the smaller tasks as follows:

- September 17 - gathered reading lists and resources
- September 20 - done reading and research
- September 22 - completed the outline
- September 25 - completed first draft
- September 28 - completed final draft (proofread and edit)
- September 30 - ready to submit

Writing these deadlines in your assignment notebook or planner will help keep you on track. It will also ensure that you do the assignment consistently over a period of time, not at the last minute. The faculty will give students a course syllabus listing all of their assignments, their due dates, and assessment weighting. Such a syllabus outline is very helpful because you can see exactly what is expected of you for the entire semester. Whenever you're given a syllabus or course structure, immediately copy the assignment question or topic into your assignment notebook or planner. Also, take note of all major exams, quizzes, and tests.

Use ring binders for handouts and lecture notes. I used to have one ring binder for each subject to file my handouts, photocopies, and lecture notes written on A-4 size or foolscap paper. Ring binders work well because you can easily insert notes and handouts, and if you ever miss a class, you can copy someone else's notes and insert them where they belong. Here's a list of basic stationeries you may need at the start of your semester.

- Ring binders for each subject
- Hole puncher
- Stapler and bullets
- Long ruler
- Five different colors of highlighters
- Red, black, and blue pens
- 2b pencils
- Eraser and corrector
- Stationery case
- Sticky note and Post-It
- Table planner with calendar
- Notebook for assignments
- Foolscap papers

File all exam, quiz, and test papers. Besides keeping all your returned assignments, also keep all of your returned papers, quizzes, and tests in the same binder with your lecture notes, or use a separate binder. Old quizzes and tests can help you revise for future tests, and they can also come in handy if there is ever a question about your grade. If you are unsure how to improve your grades or how you are doing for a subject, talk to your lecturer or advisor. As a lecturer, I welcome students to book an appointment to see me for any advice they need, and I would be happy to assist them. Your professors or lecturers are busy people, so make an appointment before you see them.

Keep a neat and organized study space. Set up a study area that consists of a desk, comfortable chair, bookshelf, and a stationery box to keep everything you need. Keep this area neat and organized so that materials can be easily located. Before you go to bed, gather everything you'll need for the following day and put everything else back in its place after use. If there's anything you need to remember to do, write yourself a note so you won't forget. You can use a small whiteboard and marker pen to write your reminders for the day.

Step 3 - Be Good in Time Management

Time management is an important skill for all college students. It is, however, particularly important for students who have other commitments such as a job, sports, and family. The first step in time management is to look at your life in order to make sure that you're not overextended. If you feel that you are doing more than you can handle, look for ways to make your life more manageable and try to make some changes.

Always plan ahead. Take a look at what you need to do, think about how you can get it done most efficiently, and then write out a plan. Revise your plans as needed, and check things off as you accomplish them. Being organized is a tremendous time-saver. When you are organized, you know what you have to do, and you have the information and materials ready.

Use your time wisely. Make smart choices about how you will use your time. For example, decide to limit yourself to one hour each day of TV, socializing, games, and social media on your phone.

Step 4 - Be Active in Class

Learn how to adapt to different lecturers. Part of your higher education is to learn how to adapt to different personalities, accents, teaching styles, and expectations of your lecturers. Some lecturers may encourage questioning, discussions, and openly exchange ideas, while others may expect students to listen to the lecture and to take notes.

Be prepared for each class. You will get more out of your lectures if you are prepared for the topic before you go to class. Lessons will be easier to follow, and you will be able to understand class discussions and get some of your questions answered. As soon as each class begins, focus on the presentation or lecture. Of course, to be physically and mentally alert, you need to eat right, exercise, and get enough sleep. If you are attending online classes, the procedures are the same, and you may get a replay of the session.

Communicate with your lecturers. Most lecturers will give you their phone numbers, email address, and/or office hours at the beginning of the semester. Do not hesitate to contact your lecturer whenever you have a concern, problem, or question. For example, if you have a paper to write, and you are having a difficult time determining how to approach the subject, talk to your tutor or lecturer. While most faculty members will be happy to help you, you must initiate the contact. You should, of course, respect your lecturer's privacy and personal time. You may talk to them after class, call or see them during their office hours, or send an email.

Be on time to class. Whenever possible, arrive early to class. You'll be more relaxed, and you can use the time to look over your notes and/or speak with your lecturer. When you are late to a class, you miss announcements and introductory remarks. Your tardiness also tells your lecturer that being on time to his/her class is not a priority for you.

Participate in class. Whenever there are discussions, projects, or labs, it is important to be an active and willing participant. The class will be more enjoyable, and you will learn more. When you participate in class, you show your lecturer and coursemates that you know the material and that you are interested in the course.

Be a good group member. The number one reason people get fired from their jobs is because they cannot get along with their coworkers. It is therefore not surprising that businesses and industries encourage educators to teach students how to work together in small groups. Here are a few things to remember when you have to do a group project:

- Do your share of the work, and do it well.
- Accept that everyone is different, and be open to new ideas.
- Have a positive attitude, and support the other group members.

Step 5 - Be Able to Take Good Notes

Be an active listener. In order to take good notes, you must be an active listener. When you are actively listening in a lecture, you don't just hear the words the lecturer is saying, you are also thinking about and trying to understand the information that is being presented.

Take notes to help you focus. You can think faster than anyone can talk. This is one of the reasons that your mind sometimes wanders when you are listening to lectures. When you take notes, however, your mind has something to focus on, and you don't have time to think about anything else. Taking notes, therefore, helps you pay attention and to stay focused. Be an active learner.

Go over your notes as soon as possible. While the information is still fresh in your mind, go over your notes. Clarify anything that was confusing, and make sure that you have keywords written in the margins of your notes. You might also want to highlight important points. Of course, while you are going over your notes, you are also fixing this information in your memory.

If you are serious about learning, completely rewrite your notes. Eliminate unimportant information, and rewrite the rest of your notes using your words. Your notes will be clearer, and as you rewrite them, you will also be learning the material and as a revision. You may try the Cornell note-taking system to take notes in lectures and in your reading.

The Cornell Note-Taking System

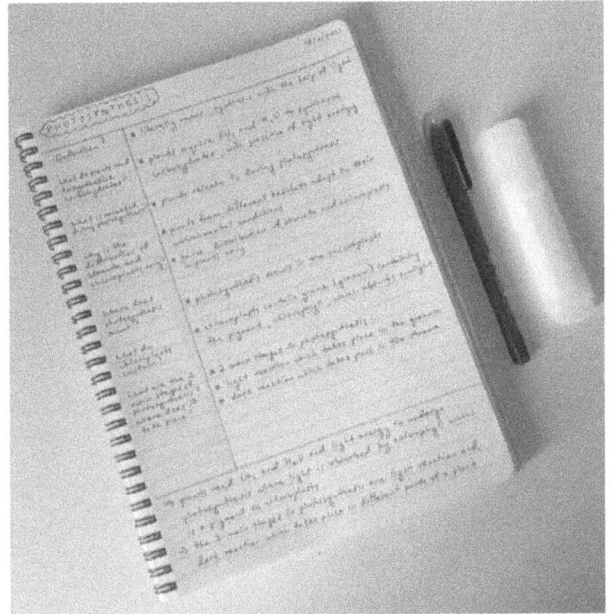

Example of Cornell Notes

Developed forty years ago at Cornell University, this system will keep your notes neat, complete, and well-organized. It will also save you time when revising for exams.

Here's an example of how to take Cornell Notes.

1. Draw a vertical line down the paper to divide the left-hand CUE column (2 1/2 inches) and the right-hand LECTURE NOTES.
2. Save the bottom two inches of the paper for SUMMARY space.
3. During class, record information only in the LECTURE NOTES area, and only on the front side of the paper.

4. Leave blank areas where you are unsure. Ask questions in class or get clarification during instructor's office hours.
5. Within twenty-four hours, review and recite from the notes. Use the Cue column to write study questions, key terms, theorems, etc.
6. In the Summary space, reduce your page of notes into a one- or two-sentence summary or mnemonic trick.
7. Quiz yourself during weekly review. Remove notepapers from the binder and spread them on a table in sequential order. Line them up so you can see only the Cue columns. Check answers in Lecture Notes.

Although you may have the freedom and independence as a student, you have to monitor your own progress as nobody will check on you whether or not you go to class or do your assignments. You are expected to study and do most of your coursework on your own, and you are fully responsible for your own academic progress and the grades you obtain. So make sure you read your college or university handbook on rules of assignment submissions, minimum passing grade, attendance requirement, and exams policy—to avoid being withdrawn from the institution.

Congratulations on your new chapter of life!

CHAPTER 4

HOW TO START YOUR NEW SEMESTER

*Motivation is what gets you started.
Habit is what keeps you going.*

—Jim Rohn

Students who *study smart* will spend less time studying, be less stressed, complete assignments faster, and get better grades. Although it is usually best to have one place to study regularly, it does not matter where you study as long as the area is well-lit, quiet, and comfortable, and there is a surface for your laptop and writing.

A library is a decent place to carry out your research and reading for your assignments while your home is a better place to write up your essay and revise for your exam. Places like Starbucks and McDonald's are not ideal for serious studying as there will be distraction from customers around. My daughter used to do her group study with friends in Starbucks before her finals, but she preferred to do all her revisions and writing at home. I let her try out what method suits her learning style best.

Before you start your semester, figure out how to avoid or eliminate anything that could interrupt your concentration, such as loud music, messages, and phone calls. Get your study corner ready. Some students need silence when they study, others can study with music playing. I used to study with my favorite songs by Roxette played in the background as motivation and sometimes instrumental music. However, I prefer classical piano music as it is soothing and makes me feel calm. If you like to listen to music when you study, consider listening to soft classical music. Research has shown that classical music can actually improve your concentration.

Get Started

The hardest part about studying is getting started. Never put your studying off until later, don't make excuses, and don't wait until you're "in the mood." Begin with something simple or a subject that you like, and just get started. We all learn differently. Think about how you learn, and adjust accordingly how you study. Here are five steps to prepare you for the new semester.

Step 1: Things to do before the term begins

Learn about study skills – It is so smart of you getting hold of this book to learn how to survive at college and, if possible, attend the available study skills workshop that most colleges and universities may organize. You can find videos on YouTube about how to study a certain subject or write an essay, and videos that teach you the skills you need every step of the way as an extension of what you learn from this book.

Read the university handbook and subject guides – Read details of the semester calendar, course structure, deadlines for assignments, exam dates, and information on sources of help (e.g., student counselors).

Scan through the course syllabus – As soon as you receive the semester course structure, read through the weekly topics, type of assignments, and suggested reading lists. Set up an *information file* to keep this and all the documents the university sends you.

Know the name of lecturer or tutor – Jot down the names of the instructors, their areas of expertise and their room location for the subjects you are taking.

Familiarize the campus – Explore the location of the faculty office, library, labs, classroom, café, hall, car park, bookshop, restroom, gym, clinic, and other facilities available at the university.

Make use of the campus library and the Internet – Spend time using the modern technology resources and facilities to boost your study. Learn about the Learning Management System (LMS) from your lecturer or any faculty members.

Step 2: Identifying your personal qualities

As a university student, you need to develop your personal qualities, such as the following:

Awareness – Know where you are starting from and what is expected of you. What do you want to achieve? Where do you need to improve? What are your current strengths and weaknesses?

Commitment – Your skills can improve through practice, reflection, and monitoring. You need to develop regular study habits in the first year.

Determination – You need to feel that you are entitled to learn and achieve. It is important that you believe success is possible, and by learning the right skills, you are to succeed as a student.

Positive thinking – You need to be clear that good study skills have little to do with being naturally clever or gifted. Success is all about strategies, practice, and confidence.

Time management – The way to study well can become a habit. Plan your time well, especially if you are not used to managing unscheduled time.

Perseverance – You must know that failure is the first step to success. Face all your difficulties by looking for solutions. Do not give up easily. There is a solution for every problem. Be resourceful.

Self-motivation – It saves you time if you have a good method to study, are disciplined, and are well organized. A skilled student uses strategies and practices them. Think about your previous personal achievement, how you overcame difficulties, and what led you to success.

Step 3: Organizing space for study

Utilize a study-only area in your room or home with your favorite furnishing so that you can concentrate on your study and manage your space better.

For example:

Personalize your space – Put up inspirational photos or posters that will motivate you, such as a vision board. It helps especially when you feel lazy or tend to give up on your work.

Organize your desk – Compile study materials in a file, and label clearly according to course or subjects. Place a calendar, stationery holder, clock, and bulletin board to post notes.

Be comfortable – Get a desk and chair that allows good posture. Proper air circulation and good lighting in your room is important.

Keep things at hand – Use a shelf for your books, files, and study materials; and tuck it next to your study desk so that you can reach them easily when needed.

Computer – Put your desktop or laptop and printer on your study desk if you do not have a side table for a computer. Avoid using the dining table for study to eliminate distractions.

Step 4: Managing your time

As a university student, you have to learn how to manage your time for tasks and personal activities. Managing your time well must become a habit if you want to be a successful student (learn more in the next chapter). Here are some quick tips on how to manage your time:

Plan a weekly study schedule – Your action plan for study is literally intended to complete your assignments and prepare for exams. Plan all the assignments for each subject according to the deadlines for submission. Get all the recommended reading lists at hand from the library or the Internet and read them. Learn the skill on how to read fast.

Example of Weekly Study Schedule

Be consistent – Sit at your desk at home or at the library, and do your assignments daily, unless you have other important things to attend to. Schedule time for study breaks, such as a ten-minute break after every hour of study.

Find time to study – Each individual has a different learning style. Some people are more alert waking up at 5:00 a.m. to study, like organizing lecture notes, reading journal articles, and making revisions. If you are not a morning person, then you may prefer to work in the evening or after midnight. Find the time that best suits you where you are most alert.

Balance between your academic and personal lives – Plan for both your study and personal time—for example, group discussion, exercise, and parties. Keep the schedule flexible for unexpected activities.

Step 5: Coping with e-learning

Many universities now incorporate e-learning to support study. How much e-learning is used varies from instructor to instructor in delivering their courses and communicating with students. The use of the Learning Management System (LMS) or Virtual Learning Environment (VLE) is common in most universities. For example, LMS or VLE can be used to deliver the following:

- Handouts for reading materials
- Course assignments or tasks
- Computer-assisted assessment
- E-communication
- Webpage and video links
- Essays or reports submission and feedback
- Assignment and exam grades

Make use of computer software and the Internet as part of your study strategy. Here are some examples:

- Use email to send messages to your tutor and other students
- Join a chat or forum for group study via Wiki and Skype
- Send your essay to your tutor through LMS
- Search information online
- Browse the Internet for research sources
- Read journal articles online
- Use PowerPoint and Google Doc to develop presentations
- Use Dropbox and Google Drive to save your documents
- Learn through videos on YouTube and podcasts
- Discuss in group via Zoom or Google Meet

Study Tips for Online Classes

With the world in a pandemic, lots of students can't go to their colleges and universities anymore. While a lot of institutions are offering online classes to their students so they can still get an education, it can still be a struggle to adjust from physical classes to online classes. Here are five study tips for attending online lectures at home, and tips for preparation and what to do after your online classes.

1. **Plan your online lectures.** You can make a distinction between prerecorded lectures and live lectures. Prerecorded lectures are lectures that have been uploaded and can be watched whenever you want. Live lectures are lectures that require your attendance at that moment; otherwise, you miss the class. For both of them, it is important to create a schedule for yourself.

First, you need to be sure how many lectures you have and when they are available to watch. If your college provides you with live online lectures only, you need to make sure that you know exactly when you have to be in the online class. If you have access to prerecorded lectures, you can generally watch these at any time.

So once you have figured out what lectures you have and when they take place, it's time to start to make a schedule that is easy to follow. You can plan your schedule on paper and put it on your desk so you can see when you have to watch your next lecture, or you can create a digital schedule and add some notifications when your next lecture is about to start. Once you have a schedule for your online lectures, it will be easier to prepare yourself.

2. **Prepare your upcoming lecture.** It is important to prepare yourself for an upcoming lecture. Depending on what you normally do, you should prepare yourself for your lecture like you normally do. Make sure to read the topic in your textbook that your lecturer may discuss in class, and also google the topic that is available online.

Preparing your upcoming lecture doesn't mean just to study related things, it also means making sure to attend your online lecture peacefully. Remind your roommates or family members to be more quiet and not bother you while you study. Tell them the time frame you need for watching your online lectures and why it is important that you need your space to be undisturbed.

3. **Avoid distractions during online lectures.** This means that you will need a work space to watch the online lectures. Pick a quiet place in your house where you can watch the online lectures without getting disrupted by other things. Otherwise, you can use headphones to create some kind of study zone to get less distracted by things around you.

It's very important that your space is neat and tidy when you are trying to study. Remove all things that you won't need, and only have the stationeries that you will need during your lecture. Also, keep a glass of water to sip, and make sure to clean your work space after your online lecture.

4. **Write your notes on paper or in digital format.** Before you attend online lectures, you need to choose between paper or digital note-taking. Both have their own benefits. Taking notes on paper makes you remember more easily, and it forces you to listen attentively to your lecturer. A laptop enables you to take notes a lot faster, so you can copy-paste

and type a lot more, but you may not be concentrating on your understanding. Besides, handwritten notes are good to make tables, drawings, and charts that are more difficult to make with a laptop.

5. **Make a quick summary of the lecture.** This will help you understand the topic or study material fast and easier to remember what you learn. Try to keep the summary of the lecture on a maximum of one piece of paper. This will keep the summary short, and you will have an overview of the most important things of the lecture. It will also be a great tool to use when you are studying for your exams later on. Last but not least, take a break and treat yourself after the online class. Also, don't forget to give your eyes a rest, because staring at your screen for a long time makes them tired.

Know Your Learning Style

Learning Style	Think by ...	Helpful Class Activities	Helpful Study Habits
Visual	visualizing	films, pictures, videos, readings, demonstrations, drawings	take notes; use flash cards, charts, diagrams; highlight important information
Auditory	hearing	lectures, discussions, videos, films, music	read aloud, have discussions, record lectures in difficult classes, use memory tricks involving rhythm and rhyme
Kinesthetic	doing	role-playing, hands-on activities, computer-aided activities, demonstrations	try moving around while you study, use tools and objects, write or type your notes

Interpersonal	discussing with others	discussion sections, organizing projects	ask questions, volunteer in class, peer tutoring
Intrapersonal	reflecting within	independent study courses	establish personal connections

Plan Your Study

Before you start to study, make a plan. Decide exactly what you want to get done and the order in which you will do it. Make sure that your plan is realistic. When I was a full-time student, I used to have a lot to do, such as juggling three part-time jobs in a week. So I prioritized my lecture and coursework to make sure I had enough time for the things that were most important. Say, if I have something to research for the next lecture, I would work on that first and then come back to read for my assignment. Use a notepad or diary to plan the stages of your assignments, revision for each subject, and group work.

Know How to Study for Tests

From the beginning of the semester, you need to study a little every day, revise and organize your lecture notes. Cramming to do everything at the last minute is very stressful. You have to know what topic you are going to cover for the test. Test questions or quizzes most often come from material that was presented in class; therefore, it is important to study your lecture notes as well as the text.

For essay tests, it is more important to understand the big picture and to know the main points and key facts. For fill-in-the-blank and multiple-choice tests, you need to know more detailed information.

Pay particularly close attention during the class before a test. Your lecturers often use this time to go over information that are going to be on the test. Ask questions when you don't understand something in class or in sections of your reading. Take notes and refer to them often as it saves time and increases your understanding. If an instructor gives you a review sheet or study guide, study it until you know everything on it, then use it to come up with questions that you think will be on the test. Also, practice past year papers as much as possible to help you get used to the format of the questions.

Get all the required readings done before you start to study for the test. If your textbook has review questions at the end of the chapters, go over them and be sure that you know the answers. You may try teaching the material to yourself or someone else. I used to talk to myself and imagined that I was teaching somebody just to test my understanding of the topic. When I was preparing for my viva voce (an oral examination to defend a thesis), my daughter was my audience, and she acted as my professor, who gave me good feedback afterward on how I spoke and my gestures.

At least two weeks before your test or exam, form a study group, take turns leading a review of the important concepts, ideas, formulas, and so on. Take turns to ask each other questions, share notes, and discuss difficult materials. Remember to use the WH questions (what, who, when, where, why, and how) for more extensive answers.

If you're feeling anxious about your future after high school graduation, you are not alone. It is totally normal to take some time for yourself to decide what you want to do next. Chase after academic success by taking proactive steps early on. Reach out to mentors, college counselors, and speak to students pursuing your major of choice. With the right preparation, you can thrive in college!

Enjoy your new semester!

CHAPTER 5

HOW TO MANAGE YOUR TIME

Time is a created thing. To say "I don't have time" is to say "I don't want to."
— Lao Tzu

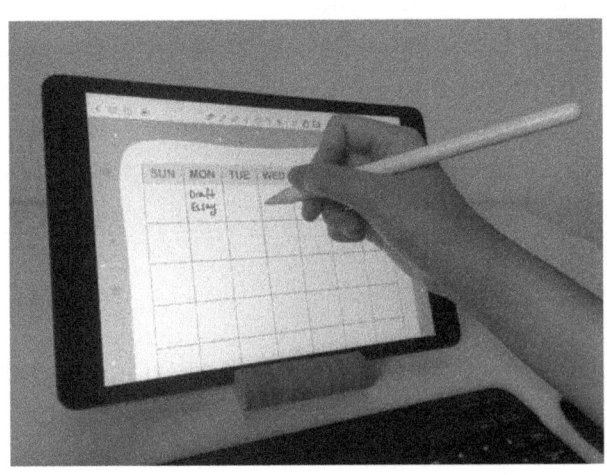

Are you spending too much time checking social media? Are you prone to texting and answering personal phone calls while studying? Do you find that a lot of time has passed while you aimlessly browse the web?

Time is a resource. Like our energy and money, time is a finite resource; and as such, it needs to be effectively managed. Time management is about planning and controlling the amount of time you spend on specific tasks. The following are some of the important skills students need to manage time effectively.

What is time management?

1. Goal-setting

It's almost impossible to use time well if you don't know what to do with it. Students can benefit from having short- and long-term goals. For example, if you are studying music, a short-term goal might include completing your reading for the assignment so you have ample time to practice music and then sit for the exam. Your long-term goal could be to represent your college in a music competition and to set up your music school after graduation.

2. Prioritization

By assessing what needs to be achieved within a given time frame, tasks can be rated according to their importance. Setting priorities for each day, week, month, and year can help students accomplish their goals. It also helps to ensure activities that are vitally important but not urgent—such as personal devotions, adequate sleep and exercise—are given precedence. Some people like to prioritize easy tasks for early in the day and use the boost to move forward. Others prefer to tackle bigger jobs first. I prioritize my tasks based on the urgency that needs to be tackled.

3. Organization

Once priorities are set, it is important to have a plan for getting them done. Some students are naturally well-organized, and others need some help. Strategies like maintaining an up-to-date calendar and keeping a tidy study environment help. There are many useful software programs and apps to aid organization. Search them up.

4. Managing stress

Nobody performs at their peak under excessive stress. Students need healthy ways to manage the pressures of study while maintaining productivity. Getting enough sleep, eating healthily, and exercising are all great ways to keep stress at bay and actually make learning more efficient.

How do you plan your day as a student?

Life as a student is busy. If you are not organized and you feel like you are not on top of things, you will be stressed. You might end up working late and sleeping less, but this is not a good idea. Getting organized for college is all about building good study habits and managing time well. Through my experiences, I have come up with five steps to manage your time that will help you to become organized, productive, and effective.

Step 1: Develop a daily routine

Being a student, you need to develop a daily routine as part of your lifestyle. Your success in everything you do lies in your daily routine. Allow yourself one hour of personal time each morning sitting quietly in the same place to do: twenty minutes of prayer or meditation, twenty minutes of reading a motivational book, and twenty minutes of exercise. Your golden hour will increase your confidence and build your good habits over time.

Consistency is the key to student success. For your study, write down your general weekly schedule and create a routine. Include things like when you will do your assignments, when you will review the things you have learned, when you will exercise, and so on. It is not possible to stick to a routine 100 percent of the time, but at least set up the framework to keep you focused and on track.

Write everything down. No one has a perfect memory, and trying to remember everything is stressful. So make a habit of writing down all your events, meetings, ideas, and things you need to do. When you write everything down, you will be less anxious because you will not be relying on your brain as a storage device.

Use a notebook or planner. Put everything in your planner: assignments, tests and exams, dates, family events, social events, exercise, and so on. This way, you will be far more organized. Try an app like Google Keep or Any.do that you can use on your phone and computer to stay organized.

Step 2: Set rules for yourself

Be disciplined, create new habits, and set some very specific rules for yourself. These could be things like taking a ten-minute break for every hour of study, completing all projects and assignments at least two days before they are due, or start revising for tests at least two weeks in advance. Make a habit of keeping one ring binder for each subject and filing your assignments and printed notes according to type. File your assignments together in sequential order, followed by your handouts or printed notes.

At the end of each week, look through all the papers, notes, brochures, and other things you have accumulated. Recycle or throw away all the things you don't need. So if you declutter once a week, you will be more likely to stay organized and easier to stay focused.

Step 3: Create your own deadline before the actual due date

Create your own deadlines and put them in your planner or calendar. Having your own deadline reduces stress for you as a student. You will also be more likely to submit your best work. Don't treat the actual deadline as the deadline. Set your own deadline one or two days before, and plan accordingly. This will help you because you probably already experience enough stress to complete all your assignments on time.

Be punctual. Wake up a little bit earlier each morning so you don't have to rush. When you rush, you often forget things, which means that your day doesn't start well. So go to bed early, get at least eight hours of sleep every night, and set your alarm so you wake up a bit earlier. For most students, waking up ten to fifteen minutes earlier is enough to avoid the unnecessary stress of rushing in the morning for personal matters. Put the alarm clock farther away from your bed so you will not be tempted to snooze.

Plan your week ahead and organize your coursework and lecture notes after each class. Test out the following websites and apps to make studying fun, keep you organized, and remove distractions so that you don't miss the deadlines: Habitica, MyStudyLife, and KeepMeOut.

Step 4: Work on one task at a time

Don't multitask, plan each assignment. Multitasking seems like a good idea because you can pretend that you are working twice as hard. We all get bored of the tasks we are working on, so jumping about seems more fun. The problem is that it does not result in the best outcomes. Breaking down big tasks and projects makes them seem less overwhelming and more manageable.

Here's what I suggest: Take a piece of paper and write down the task you are working on right now, for example, "Marketing assignment, question 1." Put that piece of paper on your study table to serve as a reminder for you to stay focused on the task at hand.

Step 5: Block out time in your schedule

Blocking out time in your schedule for the things that matter most is a crucial time-management strategy for students. If you don't do this, other things that are less important will fill your schedule. In your calendar or planner, block out time for things like family events, religious activities, volunteering, and studying. Then honor these commitments and stick to your schedule as much as possible.

If you want to make good use of your time and be an organized, effective student, you have to learn to say *no*. So decide on the boundaries you want to set for yourself. Decide how many times you will go out with your friends each week, how many days each week you will devote to family activities, and what your daily priorities are. Then practice saying no to protect these boundaries. You don't have to feel guilty when you say no! Remember, it is not about being a busy student but being an effective student.

Each week, take a few minutes to see what important events and deadlines are coming up over the next month. This will help to ensure that you don't overlook any important projects, tests, or assignments. Balancing responsibilities at your job, home, and college is not easy. No matter what, you are always left with the same twenty-four hours in a day to check items off to-do lists, spend time with family and friends, and unwind. By planning ahead and using your time wisely, you will be able to accomplish more and enjoy added free time.

Time Management Tips for Online Students

1. Plan ahead

Your hectic schedule, combined with daily distractions, can easily get in the way of finishing tasks. The best online students know how to set aside time to focus. This includes having a consistent time and work space, tuning out those distractions, and avoiding surfing the Internet unnecessarily. Despite the flexibility in being an online student, it is important to have frequent engagement with your studies throughout the week. Provide plenty of time to space out your required readings, assignments, and online discussions.

Consider purchasing a calendar or planner you can use to plan your daily and weekly assignments, highlighting

- assignments due, including drafts and final submissions;
- activities related to your program, such as study group meetups or on-campus networking events; and
- virtual or in-person office hours with professors and advisors.

Here's a sample schedule of what a typical week might look like:

Monday	Begin required readings and multimedia
Tuesday	Continue reviewing materials
Wednesday	Post to discussion forum and begin assignments
Thursday	Continue posting and working on assignments
Friday	Read and respond to posts and work on assignments
Saturday	Read and respond to posts and finish assignments
Sunday	Check your work and submit assignments

2. Don't multitask

Avoid multitasking, which can actually decrease your productivity. Focus on one assignment at a time, and zero in on the specific task at hand, whether that's studying for an exam, reading a textbook, emailing a professor, or participating in an online forum. Arrange your tasks in order of importance, and pay attention to the three or four crucial tasks that require the most effort. Concentrate on what needs to get done in the present, and avoid anything too far-off. If it is a small assignment that you don't need to address for several weeks, put it on your calendar to focus on when the deadline is closer.

3. Set up your virtual office

Whether you study at home or your local café, it is important to work in the optimal setting needed to complete your work. Make sure there is high-speed Internet and that you are in a comfortable space with the right lighting, sound, and background. For example, some people prefer to work with headphones on, while others prefer silence or an ambient backdrop with people quietly chatting or the sound of raindrops. Sit in a comfortable chair, and make sure the lighting is not too dim. Close out your browser windows, and put your phone away.

Along with these elements, make sure you have all the required materials, such as textbooks and industry-specific software. Set up as much as you can ahead of time to stay on task with your coursework.

4. Block out distractions

Make sure to avoid surfing the web excessively. It is easy to become distracted by the news or your favorite celebrity gossip site. Stay focused, and avoid Facebook, Twitter, and other social media tools when you need to concentrate on your studies.

If you're struggling to stay focused, then consider the Pomodoro Technique, a time-management method developed by Francesco Cirillo in the late 1980s. This technique helps with productivity by arranging how you work to increase efficiency. The tool builds on twenty-five-minute work sessions, optimizing your time to focus on your online studies. The best way to use this method is to

- set a timer for twenty-five minutes and work uninterrupted for the scheduled period;
- take a five-minute break to grab a coffee, check emails, or do something else; and
- once you have completed four work sessions, treat yourself to a longer, fifteen-minute break.

If you are still struggling with procrastination, download a website blocker for your Pomodoro sessions. Freedom, KeepMeOut, and Switcheroo minimize online browsing and let you follow through on your daily tasks. With these tools, you can block all websites or redirect your favorite sites to your college's homepage.

5. Reward yourself

It's important to reward yourself after a job well done in order to avoid burnout. Otherwise, it will be difficult to concentrate on even the simplest tasks. You can reward yourself by celebrating your accomplishments and treating yourself to something you truly enjoy, whether that's watching your favorite show on Netflix or going out to a nice dinner and a movie. If you have been working on an assignment for several months in a row, then take a week off when you are finished. I love this part of rewarding myself after each accomplishment. I would eat my favorite ice cream, treat myself to a nice movie, go for a massage, or buy a motivational book.

6. Create a balance

In addition to rewarding yourself, it's also important to find a balance between coursework and your other obligations, especially if you are juggling study and work.

To help create an effective balance and avoid burning out, be sure to prioritize your time in a way that allows you to focus on study, work, and your personal life when you need to. Creating a predictable schedule can help you get into a routine that works for your lifestyle and allows you to dedicate your full attention to each aspect of your life at a given time.

7. Get a good night's sleep

Sleep is essential to rest your body and keep your mind fresh for the next day. Try to get seven to eight hours of rest a night. Pulling all-nighters is less productive than studying consistently. Include sleep in your schedule, and you can reap huge rewards.

Enrolling in an online degree program is a great way to further your education and ultimately advance in your career, but it is up to you to take charge of your learning so you can get the most out of your classes. A key component of doing so is employing effective time-management strategies to stay on top of your responsibilities. Remember, time is a finite resource. So manage your time well before it manages you.

Celebrate your achievement!

CHAPTER 6

HOW TO TACKLE ASSIGNMENTS

Never leave till tomorrow which you can do today.
—Benjamin Franklin

What is a college assignment?

An assignment is a broad term, which encompasses various types of projects. Your professor or lecturer may request an essay, research paper, lab report, case study, oral presentation, programming assignment, and many other formats of academic writing.

The most important thing is to start, and start early. If you give yourself enough time to plan, research, write, and revise your work, you won't have to rush. Once you've started, you'll also have something that you can improve on.

The steps below will help you plan, research, write, and review your assignment.

How to plan your essay writing

Step 1: Identifying the task

There are basic techniques to writing an effective essay. The first thing to do before you start writing is to know what your assignment is about and make a plan. In your plan, you need to include the following:

Choose a topic – Select a topic that you are interested and familiar with based on your course or subject area. Find a general topic and narrow it down. Stick to the topic after finalizing.

Gather materials – Get all materials to support the main idea of the topic. Read about the topic from the reading lists given by your lecturer. Search and examine the books and articles from the library on campus and the Internet. Utilize the library staff who will help you with your search. Read the relevant materials using the right reading skill (see step 2).

Organize supportive evidence – Organize your ideas by making an outline. Link your supportive information or evidence to major points, and make sure there is a smooth transition between paragraphs and ideas. Put your ideas down on paper and write your first draft (see step 3).

Step 2: Improving your reading skill

Studying at the university requires you to read a lot. You will not have time to read all the books and articles on the reading lists, but you do need to have good knowledge of your subject in order to tackle the assignment. So you have to learn how to read right and fast either through books, online, or attend a workshop for reading skill. A very practical and proven method that works for me until today is the SQ3R Reading Method. This technique helps improve understanding the materials you read. The SQ3R stands for the following:

Survey – Read the introduction and summary/conclusion of the text first. Skim through the headings, graphs, figures, and keywords to get an idea of the text you read. No need to read the entire text or chapter at this stage.

Question – Identify the main points and jot down the questions you may have. Turn the headings into questions and try to answer them.

Read – Read the text or chapter and search for the answers to your questions. Scan for specific information from each paragraph, such as places, people, events, etc. Highlight the main points and keywords.

Recite – Go back over to your text and recite important names, dates, terms, examples, and so on. Jot down on paper.

Review – Check the text again for relevant points, figures, and information you need for your task. Add more notes to your paper.

How to read fast?

When you know how to read a textbook, article, and any reading material, you are able to comprehend and remember what you read. For speed-reading, you will need to do skimming and scanning as you go through the text. You may see boldface subtitles, added pictures, charts, graphs, lists of vocabulary words, numbers, and review questions in the text.

Skimming

Skimming gives you a quick overview of the materials you're going to read. To skim, read the title, the subtitles, and everything in bold and italic print. Look at all of the pictures, graphs, charts; and read the introduction, the review questions, and the conclusion or summary.

Skimming provides you with a great deal of information in a very short amount of time. In addition to providing you with an excellent overview of the text, skimming also provides you with a kind of "information framework." Having this framework of main ideas, vocabulary words, and so on makes it easier for you to read and understand the more detailed information. Ask yourself, what is the main idea of this text, and what is it about? Skim through the subtitles or the first sentence of each paragraph and the conclusion.

Scanning

When your reading has a purpose, your comprehension improves, it's easier to stay focused, and you can identify important information. To give your reading a purpose, scan through the text and turn each boldface subtitle into a question. Find out more information about those subtitles, names, and keywords in each paragraph; and keep your question in mind as you continue to scan. At the end of each section, see if you can answer it. Your question gives you something specific to look for and helps you find the details you need. Always use WH questions—such as what, why, and how—to look for more information so that you can understand and remember more of what you read.

Thus, before you start to scan a section, look to see if there are any vocabulary words, names, places, or events in bold or italic print, and then ask yourself, "Why is this word, person, place, or event important?" You should, of course, have an answer to that question when you finish reading the section. Jot down this information as you may need it for your essay, or underline the important points and write the outline of your assignment.

Review

Generally, skimming a reading material is aimed to find the idea of the text, while scanning is to get more details from the text. To review, go back to the beginning and go through the same process you did when you scanned the material. This time, as you read the boldface subtitles, briefly restate the purpose of the point of the section to yourself using your own words. As you look at the vocabulary word and the words in bold or italic print, think about what they mean and why they are significant. If you really want to lock the information into your brain, review everything again a day or two later. When you start writing your essay or sit down to study for the test, you'll be amazed at how well you already know the material.

While it may take a little practice to get the "skim, scan, review" process down, you'll soon realize that this process does not mean more work. It just means better comprehension, better retention, and academic success.

Step 3: Developing your writing

As a university student, you will frequently write lecture notes and essays, which is quite different from your general writing. You must learn *academic writing*, which presents a polished and professional image in essays, reports, research papers, and presentations, as required by the university. I have taught academic writing most of my teaching years at the university; up until today, I teach online IGCSE and IELTS English Essay Writing. Here are some helpful tips to tackle your writing tasks:

Learn Academic Writing Skill – You need to write your essay in academic style, and your lecturer expects that you possess this skill in the first semester. You may attend a workshop to develop your academic writing skill if your university does not provide the writing class in time. Nowadays, most universities offer a pre-sessional English class that teaches academic writing and oral presentation skills for foundation year or preuniversity and first-year students when the first semester starts.

Write the first draft – Use a word processor and get your ideas down with a structure that includes an introduction, body, and conclusion. Use the outline as a guide. Provide the thesis statement in the introduction, and in each new paragraph, include the topic sentence relevant to what you're going to write in that paragraph. Use the supportive evidence you have gathered to support your main points. You do not have to write the first draft perfectly. Do proofread and edit your draft for spelling, grammatical errors, word usage, and organization of points when done.

Prepare the final draft – You may revise a few more drafts before the final draft. Proofread and edit the final draft as you did in your previous drafts, and this time, make sure that it complies with the rules such as format, word count, front cover, and so on. Do not plagiarize as you will be penalized (see step 5). Submit your assignment before the deadline. If it is a group assignment, make sure all the team members complete their part to compile each section of the essay. It is easier to use Google Docs for group assignment as members may edit and post work for the group to read and edit. In the past, I introduced Wiki to my students for group collaborative writing and created a discussion forum. For instant discussion, they used Skype. But now, you have more useful apps like Google and Zoom, and download them on your phone to make studying a lot easier.

How to write an essay

The key to writing an essay is to have enough time to plan, write, and revise it. Writing an academic essay should be a process, not a one-time event. If you have a choice, choose a topic that you want to learn more about, a topic that is not too broad, and one that you already know something about. Once you have your topic, gather information, brainstorm, and, when appropriate, take a position. Make an outline, and then write a rough draft. Rewrite your essay until you have it just the way you want it, and then write the final draft.

It's important that you put your draft away once or twice during this process. When you take it out and reread it, you'll see and hear things that you didn't notice earlier; it will seem like you're reading it for the first time. Before you write your final draft, have someone else read your work to make corrections or suggestions.

To write a good paper or research dissertation, you need to

1. follow the directions exactly,
2. make sure there are no spelling or grammatical errors,
3. have someone else proofread your paper,
4. turn in a neat and clean final draft, and
5. turn it in on time.

If you have difficulty writing papers or essays, go to your college's writing tutor or hire a private tutor to guide you. Otherwise, search online and learn from YouTube videos.

Step 4: Working with the Internet

The Internet has improved the technology in communication, online entertainment, and e-commerce and is very useful for education when it comes to surfing information for learning purposes. Most universities now offer online courses for distance learning. Your lecturer may encourage students to make use of the Internet to search for extra resources. While it is an added advantage to your study, the Internet should be used wisely to boost your knowledge in your subject area. Indeed, the Internet can be utilized to assist your study. For example:

- Enhance lessons
- Research projects
- Communicate
- Search information
- Learn new skills
- Collaborate
- Make presentations
- Download software
- Save documents

However, do not rely too much on the Internet for your assignments as you need to write the essay in your own words and style. You may get some good points or ideas when you read, but you cannot copy and paste the text as if it is your own work. This is called plagiarism.

Apart from writing an essay, students will be assessed for group work and oral presentation, in addition to quizzes and exams.

How to prepare for your oral presentation

Again, I have taught this subject at the university for many years. An effective presentation is more than just standing up and giving information. A presenter must consider how best to communicate the information to the audience. Use these tips to create a presentation that is both informative and interesting:

- *Organize your thoughts.* Start with an outline and develop good transitions between sections.
- *Have a strong opening.* Why should the audience listen to you? One good way to get their attention is to start with a question as a hook, whether or not you expect an answer.
- *Define terms early.* If you are using terms that may be new to the audience, introduce them early in your presentation. Once an audience gets lost in unfamiliar terminology, it is extremely difficult to get them back on track.
- *Finish with a bang.* Find one or two sentences that sum up the importance of your research. How is the world better off as a result of what you have done?

Use these tips in preparing your presentation:

- *Design PowerPoint slides to introduce important information.* Consider doing a presentation without PowerPoint. Then consider which points you cannot make without slides. Create only those slides that are necessary to improve your communication with the audience.
- *Time yourself.* Do not wait until the last minute to time your presentation. You only have five minutes to speak, so you want to know, as soon as possible, if you are close to that limit.
- *Create effective notes for yourself.* Have notes that you can read. Do not write out your entire talk; use an outline or other brief reminders of what you want to say. Make sure the text is large enough that you can read it from a distance.

- *Practice, practice, practice.* The more you practice your presentation, the more comfortable you will be in front of an audience. Practice in front of a friend or two and ask for their feedback. Record yourself and listen to it critically. Make it better and do it again.

Use tricks when making a presentation or speech

- Use props whenever possible. Props, such as posters, pictures, books, or sorting equipment give you something to look at and something to do with your hands. You can also put notes on the back of them.
- When you give a presentation or speech, pretend that you are telling your best friend something really important.
- Effective speakers make eye contact with those in their audience. If you find this difficult to do, look at their foreheads instead.
- If you are presenting virtually via Zoom or other social media platform to a big group of audiences, then look straight on the video camera and pretend you are speaking to only one person.

During the conclusion of your presentation, reinforce the main ideas you communicated. Remember that listeners won't remember your entire presentation, only the main ideas. By reinforcing and reviewing the main ideas, you help the audience remember them.

Step 5: Detecting plagiarism and referencing

Plagiarism is an offence according to the university policy. Do not copy and paste from sources that are not your own work. This is cheating. If you need to get the ideas and points from a text to be added in your essay, then cite the text and provide the references at the end of your essay or report. The most common referencing style is the American Psychological Association (APA) Style.

The in-text citation consists of the following: author surname(s) (in the order that appears on the actual publication), followed by the year of publication of the source that you are citing. For example, *(Rowling, 2001)*. A complete reference should appear in the reference list at the end of your essay. The following are the APA format structure:

- **Cite a book in print:**
  Rowling, J. K. (2001). *Harry Potter and the sorcerer's stone.* London: Bloomsburg Children's.
- **Cite a book online:**
  James, H. (2009). *The ambassadors.* Retrieved from http://books.google.com.
- **Cite a book from a database:**
  Bloom, H. (1986). *American women poets.* Retrieved from http://www.infobasepublishing.com.
- **Cite a journal article in print:**
  Nevin, A. (1990). The changing of teacher education special education. *Teacher Education and Special Education: The Journal of the Teacher Education Division of the Council for Exceptional Children, 13*(3–4), 147–148.

- **Cite a journal article online:**
  Jameson, J. (2013). E-Leadership in higher education: The fifth "age" of educational technology research. *British Journal of Educational Technology, 44*(6), 889–915. doi: 10.1111/bjet.12103.

The difference between a reference and a bibliography is, the former is a detailed list of references that are cited in your work, while the latter is a detailed list of background readings or other materials that you have read, but not actually cited.

Have fun on your assignment!

CHAPTER 7

HOW TO COLLABORATE IN GROUP WORK

Coming together is a beginning, staying together is progress, and working together is success.
—Henry Ford

69

Why is it important for students to collaborate?

Research shows that educational experiences that are active, social, contextual, engaging, and student-owned lead to deeper learning. The benefits of collaborative learning include the following:

- Better student preparation for social and employment situations.
- Development of higher-level thinking, oral communication, self-management, and leadership skills.
- Greater student-faculty cooperation and synergy.

Why collaborative learning? I remember in my school years, we rarely had group work in class, though we participated in sports as part of a team. I learned about working in a group during class discussion and worked on one or two group assignments while studying for my bachelor's degree. The group assignment includes writing a report and performing an oral presentation. We elected a group leader and had group discussions at least once a week at the campus. Then when I became a lecturer, I taught my students how to collaborate in group work and what rules needed to be followed.

Group work is one of the most common types of student collaboration. It's also complicated and messy and never quite works out as well as we'd like. Some students feel like they're doing most of the work. Others feel left out. Motivation wanes. Assignments get cobbled together, and nobody feels like they have real ownership of the work. Here are five steps to being an effective group member:

Step 1: Ways to work with others

Some students prefer to work on their own and against working in a group. This is not the case when you are studying at the university. You will be assigned to work in a group project as part of the assessment. When working with other people, you have to contribute and allow others to contribute to the work. This is called *collaborative learning*. Being able to work effectively in groups is also a lifetime skill in the workforce. There are proper ways to work with others in a group, such as the following:

- Respect the time of team members and show up in all meetings on time.
- Respect the opinions of team members, listen, take turns, and share your ideas.
- Support each other, share responsibilities, and play your part in keeping the group running smoothly and focused.
- Use technology for communication and discussion with team members outside campus (e.g., Skype, Google Chat, Google Docs, Wiki, LMS, emails, etc.). During the COVID-19 pandemic, many universities offer online classes, and students are studying from home.

Step 2: Dealing with challenges in the group

Working in a group can be challenging, and sometimes the group fails despite all the benefits of collaborative learning. The most common reasons for group failure are unsolved conflict, free riders or social loafing, poor leadership, and common rules not being set up at the beginning when the team was formed.

There are three common types of groups formed in class or outside class:

Study group – students form a small group and meet up to study the same subject area outside class.

Class discussion or activity – group work during lecture in class about a topic as instructed by the lecturer.

Group assignment – students meet regularly to work on a project collaboratively and receive a shared grade or mark.

In this guide, group assignments will be emphasized more as it involves a team effort in collaboration for a period of time to accomplish compulsory tasks, particularly when everyone gets the same grades or marks. Here are some tips on how to deal with challenges in the group:

- If someone in your group is either lazy or incompetent, do not judge on the standard of their work. Instead, ask them if they have problems with the task and offer a solution with the rest in the team.
- If someone suggests something you don't quite understand or agree with, you can ask them to clarify or offer other suggestions.
- Some groups end up with one outspoken leader or member who interrupts others and tries to force their own ideas on them, then ends up doing everything that everyone else can't be bothered to do. Try to ensure that the burden becomes better shared if every member throws in their ideas and makes decisions together within the group.

Step 3: Speaking and listening skills

To be successful in group work, students need to know how to communicate clearly on intellectual and emotional levels. Thus, possessing good speaking and listening skills are essential to ensure smooth discussion among the team members. Effective communicators know how to

- listen carefully to others,
- explain their own ideas,
- ask questions to clarify others' ideas and emotions,
- express their feelings in an open but nonthreatening way,
- sense how others feel based on their nonverbal communication,
- initiate conversations about group climate or process if they sense tensions brewing,
- reflect on the activities and interactions of their group and encourage other group members to do so as well,
- share their thoughts, ideas, and feelings for successful group work,
- avoid unspoken assumptions and issues as these can be very destructive to group members, and
- trust one another to grow as a team.

Step 4: Preparing group oral presentation

In a degree program, students are required to give speeches or oral presentations as part of the assessment. You will be assigned to join a group project and participate in a group presentation, usually in your first year of study. Thus, you need to have the ability to speak before a big group effectively, and this is a skill you need to possess and utilize throughout your study and beyond. You may take up a course or attend a practical workshop to learn how to present and speak on stage. Giving a speech is like writing an essay as you need to use standard and formal English. How do you prepare for a group presentation?

- Discuss with your team as you would for your group essay. Organize each member to have their part to present.
- Three components of presentation—*main ideas, supporting materials,* and *transitions.*
- Collect the *main ideas* and write a detailed outline.
- Use the *supporting materials* to support main ideas or topics.
- The *transition* should help highlight the main ideas and provide the audience with a key to movement from one point to another. These transitions must be clear and prominent.
- Use your own knowledge, experience, and imagination as additional resources to your topic.
- Your speech should be expressive and natural. Do not read the speech word for word. Speak slowly and make eye contact with your audience.
- Use hand gestures, facial expressions, and questions to hook the attention and interest of your audience.
- Use PowerPoint slides, whiteboard, brochure, or materials as an aid to support your presentation.

Structure of presentation:

1. An *introductory statement* that consists of the purpose and topic of speech.

2. The *body* and main part of speech that includes the main points and supporting materials.
3. The *concluding remarks* or summary to complete the speech.

Step 5: Overcoming unfairness

"In both of the groups the other 2 people are very good friends of mine, but I just feel they're not pulling their weight. I feel so exasperated because for my part of the work I am taking my time to do the very best I possibly can and ensure that we all get a good grade, but they have a very blasé attitude towards the work and just do not seem to be trying. I think this is unfair seeing as all of our grades are dependent on how we ALL do on the group assignment."

—First Year Student

(Source: www.thestudentroom.co.uk)

Group work is an important part of a degree program at university. As a student working in a group, you may feel something is unfair and react to it as a threat. The problem is that not everyone plays by the same set of rules, possesses similar characters, attitudes, and interests. Here are some tips to help you overcome the unfairness in group work:

Be aware of what you are thinking – Catch yourself reacting in anger and frustration. Take a breath before you do anything to make the situation worse. Try to speak to the affected group member about how you and other members in the group feel. Speak with empathy and compassion. Ask how he/she would make the group work better.

Recognize what you can and cannot control – You may strongly feel the need to fight for justice, but your action requires calm, careful planning, and acting. If after talking to the affected member the situation stays the same, explain the issue to your lecturer or tutor and ask for his/her advice.

Continue the process in completing the task – There is a solution for every problem. Try to do the work together with all members in the group and encourage each other to get the task done in time. List the individual duty of who should do what, and work on it in a specific time on campus. Meet up regularly. Help each other, especially the not-so-cooperative members. Get the team leader to oversee each other's progress. Anger does not solve the problem, compassion does. If you're studying online, group discussion can be set up via Skype, Zoom, or Google Meet.

Set the golden rules

Make sure the distribution of work, what each team member's roles and responsibilities will be, is very clear to everyone. Do your best to create tasks that are interdependent, the kind that require students to work both independently and together. Set the rules at the beginning after the group is formed and elect a group leader. The group leader will oversee the performance of the group and each member's contribution to the assignment.

Online Collaboration

The work of collaborating in groups can be difficult to coordinate and challenging to complete. But it's also a great opportunity to practice communication and collaboration skills. Remember to take turns to speak when putting in your ideas to the group and say it clearly. Visual brainstorming tools, such as mind maps and virtual corkboards, can help students get organized and comfortable sharing their ideas. Though Wiki is good for asynchronous discussion for collaborative writing, below are examples of two websites you may want to try out for your group assignments:

MindMeister: This mind-mapping website has a simple interface with extensive sharing functionality. Students can browse through premade templates or build their own map by choosing a main theme and building out nodes with notes, images, attachments, and links. Bonus: Any node can contain team assignments, due dates, and email reminders, so groups can easily visualize and organize their interdependent responsibilities.

Stormboard: Students create and add "stickies" to a virtual whiteboard where group members can comment and vote. These stickies can be text, images, or videos; and users can color-code and rearrange them on the board to easily organize ideas as they brainstorm.

Every student needs to know why collaboration is important. In most workplace settings, collaboration is necessary so that you can succeed at tasks that no one person could begin to manage alone. However, collaboration online is difficult yet essential especially during the pandemic lockdown. You may find group work to be frustrating at times, but this is one of the ways to develop your interpersonal, communication, and leadership skills. You will potentially make good friends with the group members even after the assignment is submitted. Think positive and know that every problem has a solution, every difficult situation is not permanent, and this too shall pass.

All the best for your groupwork!

CHAPTER 8

HOW TO PREPARE FOR FINAL EXAMS

> Better three hours too soon than a minute too late.
> —William Shakespeare

It is essential for every school and higher institution to teach a subject called Study Skills, which can help students score in assignments and exams throughout their studies.

Final exams and semester-end papers are among the most challenging aspects of the college experience. There is so much to learn, keep organized, and remember as you head into finals. Applying effective study tips can help reduce stress and increase your grade point average.

When I was studying for my bachelor's degree, I remember how I revised for my finals in the first semester. I stayed up the whole night to memorize some terms, as I was nervous for the next day's exam. I couldn't sleep. I had plenty of coffee until morning, and my exam started at nine. The exam took two hours and when it was over, I went home and was knocked out till the evening. At that time, I didn't know how to prepare for the exams or manage my time until I learned the skills on how to study.

Here's how to prepare for your exams with five easy steps of study tips that can help you conquer your finals.

Step 1: Make a timetable or plan

When should you start preparing for your exam? Today! Never wait till the last minute or a week before the exam. Start your revision today! Know yourself, your habits, and your patterns. Try to be flexible and realistic with your strategies. Keep in control of your plans, and if it is not going well, make changes.

Make a timetable or a daily planner. Plan which subject topics you will study on which days. List tasks involved. Work in small chunks of time. Fill in your study blocks. Once you've got your schedule blocked out and you know what you need to schedule, fill in your schedule. Write down which subject you are studying in each session. This will help keep you on track, create checkpoints for the material, and allow you to organize your textbooks and study materials ahead of time. Here's what you need to do:

- Buy a daily planner or something similar. You can also use a basic notebook or desktop calendar.
- Program your schedule into your smartphone or computer.
- Download the Power Planner app, which is very useful.
- Only plan for a week at a time first, until you've figured out how your schedule works.
- Prioritize studying for approaching exams. Divide all of your studying up into the limited amount of time you have, and spread the material out over the time you have before a given exam.
- Prioritize your weakest subjects or courses that you're determined to ace.

Give yourself lots of short breaks and rewards for getting things done. Get enough sleep, do a bit of exercise, meditate daily, and eat some healthy energy food. Drink lots of water!

Step 2: How do you revise?

Effective revision is not something that can be rushed. The earlier you start and the more organized you are, the greater your chance of success. It helps to be as realistic as possible when you plan for exam revision. Use proactive strategies to identify a key topic. Use Mind maps (my favorite method). Identify what you don't know, and find the answers. Ask yourself the WH questions, and write the answers in your own words.

Look over your syllabus and decide how you're going to approach your revision. Find out the format for your exam as this will determine how much of the syllabus you need to revise. There are various revision techniques, including flash cards, past papers, mind maps, group work, and recording yourself talking and playing it back (I used this method too). There's an element of trial and error to finding what works for you, and bear in mind what works well for one exam may not be the best method for another.

It's a good idea to have a routine with your revision where you aim to start and finish at roughly the same time each day. Try and revise in the morning as this is when your brain is fresher.

Step 3: Useful revision activities

Some students prefer to study all by themselves while others like to study in a small group. It is helpful to discuss difficult questions with your peers and exchange answers. In a group study, talk through an answer to a question, such as, What does this mean? How does it relate to x?

Working with your peers can help keep the revision process in perspective. Everyone can share revision material and plans. Listening to how others approach their revision can expand your understanding of the topics because everyone brings their own ideas and their own ways of comprehending the topics. You may find that one person is good at devising a manageable revision timetable while another has valuable ideas about content for a tricky past exam question. Besides, what one person forgets, another may remember. You are not in competition with your peers taking the exam, so sharing each other's ideas in revision is not cheating.

After your group study, organize your notes around particular questions, issues, themes; and rewrite your notes to clarify ideas and to remember what you have revised.

Step 4: Organizing and using notes

Your lecture notes are helpful for exam revision. Try to rearrange and organize your notes after class on the day itself. Sort through and highlight what is essential, and reduce notes to key headings, points, and references. Make flash cards with key points to trigger memory. Try using colored paper so that all related notes are made on sheets of the same color. Some notebooks have sections in different colors and give the advantage of keeping all your notes in one place. Alternatively, you can use pens or highlighters of different colors for different sections or topics for your notes.

If you use a computer, smartphone, or tablet to type your notes, you have to name the folders clearly to indicate their content, and use subfolders if it helps to keep your notes tidy. Digital notes are as good as written notes nowadays due to more online classes going on. However, when you go paperless, taking notes is easy, but knowing what to do with them is hard. You need to know how to organize and store your digital notes in a way that makes them useful for exam revision. The note-taking apps, free or paid, that are popular among students are as follows:

- Microsoft OneNote, if you want a free note-taking app

- CollaNote, a free practical app (my daughter is using this app)
- Evernote, if you don't mind paying for a Premium subscription
- Notability, a paid app and in-app purchases
- GoodNotes, a paid app without in-app purchases
- Quip, use for collaborative note-taking

Think carefully about where to keep your notes and how to store them so they are easily accessible. Organizing your notes and keeping them tidy will save you time for your exam revision.

Step 5: Use past exam questions

Preparing for your exam in advance will give you more time to relax the night before the exam and less stress. Regular practice in answering past year exam questions is also good preparation. Try to ask your lecturer for samples of past year's paper. Find links between exam questions and areas of study. Plan for exam essays and time yourself to make sure that you are managing your time well. Do at least one timed "exam" essay with a friend, then discuss each other's essay.

Doing past papers helps you understand what they look for in an answer. In this way, you can see what points get awarded for and understand the allocation of marks and marking scheme. Moreover, you will get used to the structure of a paper and the language they use. It's a good way to practice writing while working on your time management and to finish the paper before the time's up.

Other techniques for exam revision

Not every studying technique works for every student, so experiment with a few of these important study tips to find out which ones work best for you.

Here are twenty tips to prepare for your finals:

1. Create your own study guide.

While many teachers provide a study guide, creating your own can help you understand the material better. Outlining the important information you need to learn can be helpful, both in creation and to refer to during your studies.

2. Ask questions.

Your tutors, professors, and college counselors are there to help! Ask them questions regarding the material and the exam so that you're prepared when test time arrives.

3. Attend the review session.

In-person or virtually, review sessions offer vital information you want to know about. Including exam format, important topics, and key concepts you should be focusing your studies on.

4. Start early.

Know your final exam schedule. If you always start ahead of schedule, you'll never be cramming the night before an exam. You'll almost always perform better in doing so!

5. Organize a socially distanced group study session.

It can be helpful to study in groups sometimes. Evaluate whether or not studying with others will be beneficial to the subject as well in your learning process. Consider setting up a Zoom meeting or a Facebook chat to embrace social distancing.

6. Study the stuff not on the study guide.

Study guides aren't always comprehensive—they're just suggestions of the main concepts to learn. Use your study guide for its intended purpose: a guide. Be sure to fill in the blanks with related information.

7. Take breaks.

You won't be able to memorize or comprehend all the material at once. Balance is key, so ensure that you reward learning with break times to relax and recharge.

8. Stay well-rested.

There's a lot to be said about a good night's sleep. Make sure you're well-rested so that you can be fully focused during your exams.

9. Create a study schedule and follow it.

Splitting the material into chunks that you can actually achieve can be very beneficial. That way, you can keep track of what you've accomplished instead of looking at the big picture and getting overwhelmed.

10. Prioritize your study time.

Some exams will be more difficult than others, some you may find easier to study for. Some may be worth more of your grade than others. Make sure to evaluate all of your exams to consider and determine all of the involved factors so you can study accordingly.

11. Study for the style of the exam.

An effective study technique is to practice the exam as it will be delivered. If it's multiple choice, you'll need to know definitions and concepts. For essay exams, focus on your understanding of all the concepts presented, with examples in mind.

12. Quiz yourself.

If you think about and create actual exam questions, you will likely become more familiar with what you need to study and, in the meantime, familiarize yourself with the type of language that will be on the exam. Draft potential exam questions and quiz yourself so that you can set expectations of what you need to focus on.

13. Meet with your professor or tutor.

Oftentimes, meeting with an instructor can give you helpful hints for what to study and ways to prepare for the exam. Consider sending him/her an email to see what the best way to connect is for them. Be prepared for a virtual meeting request during the COVID-19 pandemic.

14. Reorganize your notes.

Evaluate and reorganize your notes into what's important, outlining important concepts, formulas, dates, and definitions so they're easy to understand.

15. Pace yourself.

Make sure you stay focused and don't burn yourself out. A great way to do so is to pace yourself. Learning retention won't work well if you're studying for long periods of time. In the long term, it's best to study in short periods. Take a break, reset, and study some more for final exam week.

16. Teach classmates.

Learning by teaching is a method that really works! If you work with a study buddy and explain concepts to each other, you're relearning the material all over again. It's a great way to reinforce what you've learned and help someone in the meantime! Just plan ahead to avoid pulling an all-nighter cram session.

17. Revolve your focus.

Switching up your subjects is a helpful way to learn everything for your exams while preventing burnout on one topic. Make sure to switch it up before your eyes glaze over! That way, you can keep studying for longer periods of time while maintaining your focus.

18. Color-code it.

Create a system that allows you to color-code material that's going to be on the exam by what's most important, less important, etc. This will help you focus on the most pertinent information and prioritize the material.

19. Visualize.

If you're a visual learner, it can help to create mind maps or diagrams to visualize how the concepts you're learning relate to one another. This is especially beneficial when learning concepts that build upon the understanding of one another, like in science courses.

20. Make it fun.

It's easier to focus if you adapt your final exam studying techniques. Consider quizzing yourself, creating acronyms, then rewarding yourself for a job well done.

Questions Commonly Asked by College Students

Here are some of the questions you may ask:

When should I start studying for finals?

The best time to start studying is at the beginning of the class. Set aside a little time each week to sit down and organize your notes and think about what's going well and what's going badly. Three to four weeks ahead of time is the latest that you want to create an exam study plan for yourself.

How many hours should I study for a final exam?

If you have kept a good daily and weekly schedule, fifteen to twenty hours should be about right for a midterm, twenty to thirty for a final exam. Major papers take substantially more time and effort.

How can I crack my exam in one month?

Follow these four tips to crack competitive examinations:

Step 1: Follow a timetable. As a first step, make a timetable keeping in mind what you want to achieve in the short-term and long-term.

Step 2: Focus on preparation.

Step 3: Evaluate yourself.

Step 4: Stay positive and confident.

Is one hour of studying enough?

University experts recommend two to three hours of studying per one hour of class. Following this method can result in a very, very long day for the average college student. You can use this method if it works for you, but in reality, it's all about knowing you and how you study.

What is the best time to study?

Although new discoveries prove that timing may not be everything, it is important if you want to create and perform at your best consistently. That said, science has indicated that learning is most effective between 10:00 a.m. to 2:00 p.m. and from 4:00 p.m. to 10:00 p.m., when the brain is in an acquisition mode.

Is studying at 4:00 a.m. good?

A study by the University of Westminster found that people who wake up early (between 5:22 a.m. and 7:21 a.m.) have higher levels of a stress hormone than those who have a leisurely morning, and yet many successful people are early risers. It is good if you sleep at 9:00 p.m. so that you can get up and study at 4:00 a.m.

What do top students do?

Top performing students take far more practice tests than their peers, and doing so helps the student move beyond just memorizing material. Another key skill was not just working hard. Top students do work hard, but the research showed that many students who worked just as hard or harder didn't perform as well.

What can help memory naturally?

Here are important evidence-based ways to improve your memory naturally:

- Eat food with less added sugar
- Try a fish oil supplement
- Make time for meditation
- Maintain a healthy weight
- Get enough sleep

- Practice mindfulness
- Drink less alcohol
- Train your brain

Review returned tests

When your test is returned to you, go over each question you missed, and if possible, write in the correct answer. You may see one or more of these types of questions on your final exam. Also check to make sure your test was graded correctly (mistakes happen). Keep a record of your test scores, and keep all of your returned tests in a file or folder.

Remember, stress and fatigue can grow when your exam is closer. Avoid last-minute revisions! Take good care of yourself in the days leading up to exams. Get enough rest for at least six to eight hours of sleep a night. Eat regularly and don't skip meals in order to study. Eat healthy and don't overload on junk food or caffeine. Take breaks and exercise. Visualize your success—imagine yourself writing a good essay and feeling successful. Relax, smile, and breathe.

Come on, you can do it!

CHAPTER 9

HOW TO REMEMBER WHAT YOU LEARN

> I hear and I forget. I see and I remember.
> I do and I understand.
>
> —Confucius

I believe in doing our best. Not everyone needs a straight A result as most of us are average people. We don't have to strive too hard to achieve a top score beyond our ability, but if you are determined to be successful, you will study smart to pass the exams and graduate. Your focus should be the process, the journey toward your goal, not the product or the result itself. Although you may dream with the end in mind, and see yourself achieving your goals, you need to pay attention to the what rather than the how. What do you want? My answer: I want to be highly educated so that I can educate others. What are you going to do? My answer: I'm going to get a degree and teach tertiary students.

When I was a university student, I thought studying to get good marks was the only option I had because that was what I experienced in Malaysian schools. Over the years after graduating with a degree, I realized that the aim to be successful in studying is not exactly the end result itself. It is the process and the journey of getting things done that brings the results we desire. This is what I did as a postgraduate student. I always prepared for the next lesson and attended classes 100 percent in the first semester. I read all the suggested reading lists and bought any recommended reference texts for the subject. At that time, there wasn't much about online journals and e-books; hence, the university library used to be like my second home. So after the first semester of studying for a master's degree, I applied for a scholarship offered by the university, and I got it. My fees were all paid for, and I also received allowance for books and stationeries. When you focus better, you will feel more motivated to study and get the results you want. Despite that, students will have piles of materials to read for their assignments and exams. How do you remember what you read and learn?

Here are six steps to study more effectively and remember what you learn.

1. Study the material repeatedly in different ways

Research shows that different media stimulate different parts of the brain (Willis 2008). The more areas of the brain that are activated, the more likely it is that you'll understand and retain the information. Read, listen, write, and say it to remember what you learn, such as a text, a term, a formula, and so on. For instance, to learn a specific topic, you can do the following:

1. Read the lecture notes, recommended textbooks, and journals
2. Look up online resources like videos and podcast on the topic
3. Create a mind map on the topic
4. Teach someone what you've learned about the topic in a peer group

Of course, you won't be able to do all of these things in one sitting. So each time you review the topic, use a different resource or method, and you'll learn faster and remember more this way.

2. Take notes by hand instead of typing on your laptop

Scientists recommend this, and not just because you're more likely to give in to online distractions when using your laptop. Even when laptops are used only for note-taking, learning is less effective (Mueller and Oppenheimer 2014). Why? It's because students who take notes by hand tend to process and reframe the information. In contrast, laptop note-takers tend to write down what the lecturer says word for word, without first processing the information. Therefore, students who take notes by hand perform better in tests and exams.

3. Review the topic consistently

Reviewing the topic that you learned periodically is essential if you want to move information from your short-term memory to your long-term memory. This will help you get better exam grades. A research study indicates that periodic review beats cramming, hands down (Cepeda et al. 2008). The optimal review interval varies, depending on how long you want to retain the information. For example, I say at least three to five review intervals would be sufficient for each subject in a semester.

First review: one day after learning a new topic, organize your lecture notes

Second review: three days after the first review

Third review: seven days after the second review

Fourth review: twenty-one days after the third review

Fifth review: thirty days after the fourth review

4. Focus on the process instead of the outcome

Successful students focus on learning the topic, not on getting the highest grade. Stanford psychologist Carol Dweck's research shows that these students concentrate on effort rather than the end result, and they focus on the process, not on achievement. As a student, you have to believe that you can improve even in your weakest subjects and put in the time and effort to learn. Successful students set learning goals while the not so successful tend to set performance goals. Concentrate on the learning process. When you learn the right way, your performance soars.

Here are some tips on how to remember information:

- Use flash cards to memorize vocabulary words, facts, and lists. (I used this too)
- Write down what you want to memorize and concentrate on it. Close your eyes and try to see it in your mind. Say it, and then look at it again. (I did this)
- Use as many senses as possible. For example, if you write out what you want to remember and, at the same time, say it out loud, you are simultaneously hearing it, seeing it, and physically involved in the writing of it.
- Look for ways to recognize information. Draw diagrams, graphs, and pictures; make outlines, lists, and charts.
- Before you go to sleep, go over any information that you want to remember. Your brain will process this information and commit it to memory while you sleep.
- Use acronyms to help you memorize.
- Use the first letter of words you want to remember. For example, HOMES can help you remember the Great Lakes (Huron, Ontario, Michigan, Erie, and Superior). (My daughter loves this method)
- Look for a logical or an easy connection. For example, to help yourself remember that Homer wrote the *Odyssey*, just think to yourself, "Homer is an *odd* name."
- Use silly associations and ridiculous visual images to help trigger your memory.

- Review is the key to learning anything. When you are reviewing, you move information from your short-term memory into your long-term memory.
- Teaching others the material you are learning is an extremely effective method of retaining information. (I used this method for all my degrees)

5. Simplify and summarize the topic

Try to use mnemonic devices like acronyms to simplify the terms, as these are proven to increase learning efficiency. My daughter did this, and she found it very useful in boosting her memory before her exams. Choose what suits your learning style.

For example, in order to increase frequency, the electromagnetic spectrum is: **R**adio, **M**icrowave, **I**nfrared, **V**isible, **U**ltraviolet, **X**-rays, **G**amma rays.

If you want to memorize the electromagnetic spectrum, you could use this acronym/sentence: **R**aging **M**artians **I**nvaded **V**enus **U**sing **X**-ray **G**uns.

Another example is the following:

Question: Stalactites and stalagmites—which ones grow from the top of the cave and which ones grow from the ground?

Answer: Stalac**t**ites grow from the **t**op, while stala**g**mites grow from the **g**round.

Study smart by using mnemonic devices whenever possible. In addition, you could summarize the topic into a comparison table, diagram, or mind map. These tools will help you learn the topic much faster.

6. Test yourself regularly

In your learning process, you need to test yourself regularly to ensure that you remember what you learned. Decades of research has shown that self-testing is crucial if you want to improve your academic performance. Most colleges and universities offer quizzes to test students' learning before the finals.

In one experiment, University of Louisville psychologist Keith Lyle taught the same statistics course to two groups of undergraduates. For the first group, Lyle asked the students to complete a quiz at the end of each lecture. The quiz was based on material he had just covered. However, for the second group, Lyle didn't give the students any quizzes. At the end of the course, Lyle discovered that the first group significantly outperformed the second on all four midterm exams.

As a general rule, the more senses you involve and the wider variety of methods you use while studying, the more you remember. William Glasser, author and expert in the field of education, says that "students learn 10% of what they read, 20% of what they hear, 30% of what they see, 50% of what they see and hear, 70% of what is discussed with others, 80% of what they experience personally, and 95% of what they teach to someone else."

Last but not the least, don't just passively read your textbook or your lecture notes. Study smart by quizzing yourself on the key concepts and equations. As you prepare for a test, do as many practice questions as you can from different sources. Remember, the foundation of your success lies in what you believe you can do.

Do your best!

CHAPTER 10

HOW TO HANDLE RELATIONSHIPS

> Surround yourself with only people who
> are going to lift you higher.
> —Oprah Winfrey

I flew thousands of miles away from my parents and siblings to live and study in England. All I had at that time was my boyfriend, and I was homesick for three months, crying myself to sleep every night. I didn't have my family with me though I called them every festive season. Then I got myself new jobs while studying to keep myself busy for years. I also met a number of good friends at work.

How do relationships impact academics?

A relationship can vacillate between being a source of support and being an additional source of stress. Being a student, it is important for you to identify where a particular relationship falls on the stress-support continuum and to set boundaries accordingly in order to prevent decline in your study.

An interpersonal relationship refers to the association, connection, interaction, and bond between two or more people. There are many different types of relationships. I will focus on the four basic categories of interpersonal relationships: family, friends, romantic partners, and colleagues.

It is important to surround ourselves with family and friends for support and comfort in both times of joy and distress. Studies have shown that having supportive relationships is a strong protective factor against mental illnesses and helps to increase our mental well-being. Despite that, friendships and familial relationships can be both a source of stress and a source of comfort depending on the circumstances. Whatever your own unique relational balance is amongst your friends and/or family members, know that both friends and family can provide meaningful and fulfilling connections.

Family vs. Friends

When it comes to comparing friendships and familial relationships, know that the quality of the relationship is a key component of how meaningful, supportive, and fulfilling a relationship is. This means that whether you are mostly close to your friends or your family, you can still experience loving, healthy, and respectful relationships.

So what does it mean to have a supportive network of family and friends?

It is about building and maintaining a network of people that you can trust and fall back on in times of difficulty. For example, I needed money to fulfil my dreams and goals to study for a degree. My sister and my boyfriend were willing to help, and I worked to pay them back with gratitude. When you borrow money, you have to be genuine and determined in achieving your goals, not for the sake of borrowing money to try out something. If you want to try something to see whether it works for you, then I suggest you work and save some money to do it or use your credit card if you have one. You must possess the feelings of appreciation when someone helps you when you need them in times of difficulty.

Why is it important to have a supportive network of family and friends?

We need to feel a sense of belonging to a larger social group and feel socially connected to our family and friends. For instance, my family was far away from me when I was in England, and I didn't have any relatives around. My boyfriend was the closest to me. Living in a foreign country, I had to meet new people, colleagues, and coursemates to have a sense of belonging in the society. Furthermore, I needed people to turn to for advice and encouragement whenever I faced difficulty. If you are staying with your family or living in your own country while you're studying, then you may already have a sense of belonging to a familiar group of family and friends.

It is not enough to just have one person in your support network as you may over-rely and exhaust that person. For example, my boyfriend and I looked after each other through thick and thin, and we relied so much on each other. However, we had our housemates and coursemates from campus to socialize with; we also had the best landlord (Irish) and the family who treated us like we truly belonged there. Yet it can also be devastating if the only one person that you have been relying on is unable to be with you. Therefore, it is advisable to have a number of strong relationships in your social circle.

Boy-girl relationships at college

Keeping up a boy-girl relationship whilst at university can be difficult. When you are in a relationship, your priorities change, and you want to be with the person you love all day long. Of course, this is not meant in a negative way, but having said that, it can still be challenging to combine having a relationship with your studies. Being in love is amazing, and your boyfriend or girlfriend can make you the happiest one in the world. I suggest that you follow these simple tips to make sure your bae stays your bae:

- Tell each other when you need to study. If you don't tell him/her that you need to study, they won't know it, so they will keep bothering you while you're working.
- Plan your dates. Make appointments when you are going to see each other and stick to it. If you're living with your partner, have a study date once in a while.
- Do a study session using FaceTime if you are in a long-distance relationship. It is very motivational to see the other person work, and it is nice to have a study buddy.
- Help and support each other. An important part of being in a relationship is to get the best out of each other. Help to make the other person feel more confident about his/her capabilities and to make sure the other person is exam ready.
- Trust and respect each other's privacy and personal time with family and friends, or some "me" time.

Remember that being in a relationship is more than just love, you are a team. I think most of the people in a relationship are very serious about it and want a future together. They tend to forget what they aimed for initially. I was living with my boyfriend who was also a university student. It was crucial for both of us to do our absolute best in order to get the happily ever after we deserved. Even though not all relationships last, your education is something no one can ever take away from you. Do not give yourself the excuse that "you were heartbroken; therefore, you dropped out blaming your ex!" Michelle Obama said, "There is no boy, at this age, cute enough or interesting enough to stop you from getting an education. If I had worried about who liked me and who thought I was cute when I was your age, I wouldn't be married to the president of the United States."

How healthy is your relationship?

Consider the following questions for all of your relationships.

Balance

- Do you both maintain and respect healthy boundaries?
- Do you both feel free to express an opinion?
- Does your relationship allow for change and growth?
- Does your relationship get in the way of your study, work, or other commitments?

Trust

- Are you honest with each other?
- Are you able to be yourself when you are together?
- Does your partner/family member/friend say one thing but mean another?
- Can you depend on each other?

Respect

- Do you treat each other with respect and kindness?
- Is either of you overly negative or critical?
- Has either of you ever acted in a threatening manner?
- Do either of you have a problem controlling anger?
- Do you argue on a regular basis?
- Do either of you have a problem with alcohol or drugs?

Support

- Are you gaining something positive from the relationship?
- Do you feel cared for and valued?

- Does spending time together make you happy?
- Is time spent with friends and family encouraged and respected?

Communication

- Is there equal and open communication in the relationship?
- Do you ask for each other's opinions?
- Do you listen to each other and try to see things from the other's point of view?
- Do you share helpful information with each other?
- Does each of you share a genuine interest in what the other has to say?

How to handle conflict

Conflict in a relationship is normal, but how you handle the conflict can make or break a healthy relationship. If you handle the conflict in a positive way, you can diffuse the anger and come to common ground, a win-win situation. However, if you argue unfairly, you will not reach a compromise, and neither of you will be happy. Here are some common pitfalls to avoid in conflict resolution, as well as tips for positive communication during disagreements.

Common pitfalls

- Refusal to listen to the other's point of view
- Using disrespectful language or name-calling
- Assuming you know the other person's motives or thoughts
- Refusal to compromise

- Bringing up past events to fuel the argument
- Refusal to apologize
- Arguing when you are too angry
- Planning what you are going to say next while the other is talking

Tips for positive communication

- Be open to hearing the other person's point of view, even if you disagree.
- Show your partner/family member/friend you're listening by restating what you heard him or her say.
- Avoid blame and judgment.
- Allow the other person to explain and don't interrupt.
- Discuss the issue without bringing up the past.
- Admit you're wrong; saying you're sorry can go a long way toward solving conflict.
- If you are angry, give yourself time to calm down before talking.
- Really listen to the other person and calmly respond to his or her points.
- Attack the problem, not each other.
- Be willing to give and take.

Remember that in a relationship, happiness always comes first. To make each other happy, you must not stop each other achieving your individual goals, and make sure you build your own separate, fulfilling lives. Your partner should improve your life, not be your life, and vice versa. Having a supportive network of family and friends can also help us to be positive when we go about our daily life.

Nevertheless, if you are in an unhealthy relationship, whether it's your partner, parents, siblings, boss, or friends, for instance, if they are narcissistic, then you have to leave them as fast as you can. Narcissistic means having or showing an excessive interest in or admiration of oneself and one's physical appearance. Narcissistic personality disorder (NPD) is one of several types of personality disorders. Narcissistic people have a hard time seeing another person's point of view, and they can never love another person but themselves. The way they speak and manipulate you can really drive you crazy. I know very well how a narcissist is, but I will not discuss it here. I suggest you search it up and read about it to find out the traits and signs so that you can avoid living or dealing with a narcissist.[1]

How to say NO

To many, saying no to a certain favor or a task isn't as easy as you might think.

Without communicating the right way, it can often ruin any friendships or relationships. However, rejecting others to do something that doesn't seem right or is uncomfortable for you isn't always easy. We usually feel pity for the other person when we can't help them, and some people would think it's rude to reject people's offers or invitations. So what should one do in these situations? How to say no politely to anybody such as your friends, classmates, family, associates, sellers, etc.?

Here are five common ways for you to say *no* in a polite manner:

---

[1] https://www.helpguide.org/articles/mental-disorders/narcissistic-personality-disorder.htm

1. I'm honored, but I can't (when you are invited to a party or any formal events)
2. Unfortunately, now is not a good time (when you are asked to join an activity, make a contribution or buy something)
3. Sorry, I'm booked into something else right now (when you are invited to participate in a charity or any holiday or weekend functions)
4. No, thank you, but it sounds lovely, so next time (when you are invited for a movie or a day out for social gathering)
5. Thank you so much for thinking of me, but I can't (when you are invited to your favorite places or meals or hobbies)

Keep in touch with friends and loved ones on a regular basis. Make an effort to catch up over a cup of coffee or even a simple phone call to ask them about how they are getting on. By putting in the time and effort to maintain your relationships, you will enjoy the positive returns from the strong connections you have with the people in your life. Always remember your priority—to achieve your big dreams and goals you have set.

Tie yourself to your goals, not to people. Good luck!

CHAPTER 11

HOW TO LIVE A HEALTHY LIFE

> Ask for what you want. Believe that you deserve
> it, and then allow life to give it to you.
> —Louise Hay

College is a time of dramatic changes. For some students, it's the first time that they're independently living on their own with the responsibility to finally take charge of their own life. College courses are also much more difficult than any other previous schooling, leading to burning midnight oil to study and huge amounts of stress. Unless you're living with your parents and eating home-cooked meals, it's easy for new college students to feel overwhelmed and pick up some unhealthy eating habits; but with a little preparation, you're certain that your health is up to the challenge.

When I was studying in England, I used to have five mugs of coffee throughout the day. When stress took over, I joined my housemates for a fag (British slang for *cigarette*) to release tension. After my first year, I stopped smoking as it didn't help my concentration in the long run, and it wasn't healthy at all. Instead, I chose relaxing music and watching a movie when I was feeling stressed and burned out. During the winter, I gained a lot of weight, and I wasn't eating right or doing any exercises for a healthy and fit body. I skipped breakfast whenever I had a morning lecture, and my first meal of the day would be lunch at noon—a banana, sandwiches, and a cup of coffee. Then I would stuff my stomach at dinner because I was starving. It was not a healthy lifestyle. I started to search and learn about nutritious food and the type of exercises that can boost my energy mentally and physically.

We know that eating a balanced diet, exercising, and getting plenty of rest are key to maintaining good health. However, that can seem to be an impossible task while in college. Frequently, the appeal of sweets, fast food, caffeine, and alcohol outweigh healthy options when you're in the company of friends or under stress from coursework.

Here are some important tips that are easy to follow in three main categories to maintain an energetic and healthy student lifestyle.

1. Nutrition

Eat a variety of nutritious foods. Your body actually needs more than forty different nutrients for good health, and there is not one single source for them. Your daily food selection should include a balance of good carbs, protein, fruits, veggies, and dairy products.

Eat moderate portions. If you keep portion sizes moderate and reasonable, it is easier to eat what you want and maintain a healthy and balanced diet. What's a moderate portion? A medium-sized piece of fruit is one serving. A cup of pasta equals two servings, and a pint of ice cream contains four servings. It's all about portion control!

Don't skip meals. Skipping meals can lead to out-of-control hunger and frequently results in overindulging. Snacking between regular meals can help if you are pressed for time. Just make sure you have at least two balanced meals.

Don't eliminate certain foods. Since our bodies require diverse nutrition, it's a bad idea to eliminate all salt, fat, and sugar from our diets, unless told to do so by our doctor. Choosing options such as skim or low-fat dairy will help you maintain a balanced diet.

Drink filtered water. Stay away from Cokes and other sugary sodas, which can pack as much as seventeen teaspoons of sugar per 20 oz. drink! Sugar is a source of empty calories that can use up important vitamins and minerals in your body. Water helps not only to hydrate but also to aid in blood circulation, the removal of toxins from our bodies, and in the regulation of our body temperatures.

Avoid too much caffeine. Caffeine is a mildly addictive drug that can affect your ability to sleep and focus while also affecting such bodily functions as muscle function and the cleansing of waste products. My daughter drinks rooibos tea, which contains nutritional benefits with rich antioxidants.

Drink at least eight glasses of water a day. You probably think you drink enough water, but studies show that up to 75 percent of people are in a chronic state of dehydration. Dehydration is bad for your brain, and your exam grades too.

A research study led by Dr. Caroline Edmonds of the University of East London School of Psychology found that your brain's overall mental processing power decreases when you're dehydrated. The simple solution? Bring a water bottle wherever you go, and make it a habit to drink water before you start to feel thirsty.

Eat omega-3 fatty acids. Omega-3 fatty acids are critical for brain function. One experiment found that taking a combination of omega-3 and omega-6 fatty acids can reduce test anxiety in students and improve their mental concentration (Yehuda 2003).

Omega-3 fatty acids are linked to the prevention of high blood pressure, heart disease, diabetes, arthritis, osteoporosis, depression, attention deficit/hyperactivity disorder (ADHD), dementia, Alzheimer's, asthma, colorectal cancer, and prostate cancer.

Here are foods that are rich in omega-3 fatty acids:

- Salmon
- Sardines
- Mackerel
- Trout
- Flaxseed
- Pumpkin seeds
- Walnuts

If you're a vegetarian, there are alternatives to getting choline in your diet:

- Lentils
- Sunflower seeds
- Pumpkin seeds
- Almonds
- Cabbage
- Cauliflower
- Broccoli

Best foods to boost your brain and memory

- Fatty Fish
- Coffee
- Blueberries
- Turmeric
- Broccoli
- Pumpkin seeds
- Dark chocolate

- Nuts
- Oranges
- Eggs
- Green tea

Skip your takeaway foods during the week, and have a six-day meal plan. Here are some of the simple, easy-to-cook, and delicious recipes you want to try. You can cook more for each meal to pack in the fridge and consume for six days. You may get your grocery and cook your meal prep on Sunday for the following week. This way, you are actually saving time and effort to cook every day. Check out other recipes from the link provided.

Breakfast

Overnight Oats[2]

Ingredients (1 serving)

1/2 cup rolled old-fashioned oats

1/2 cup milk of choice

1/4 cup nonfat Greek yogurt

1 tablespoon chia seeds

1 tablespoon sweetener of choice, honey or maple syrup

1/4 teaspoon vanilla extract

---

2 https://feelgoodfoodie.net/recipe/overnight-oats/

Topping—Banana Nutella

1/2 banana, sliced

1 tablespoon Nutella

1 tablespoon hazelnuts, crushed

1 tablespoon chocolate chips

Instructions

1. Place all ingredients into a large glass container and mix until combined.
2. Cover the glass container with a lid or plastic wrap. Place in the refrigerator for at least two hours or overnight. Toppings can be added the night before or immediately before serving.
3. Uncover and enjoy from the glass container the next day. Thin with a little more milk or water, if desired.

Lunch

Spaghetti Bolognese[3]

Ingredients (6 servings)

2 x glugs of oil—olive, vegetable, or sunflower

250 g mushrooms, chopped

---

[3] https://www.goodhousekeeping.com/uk/food/recipes/a535269/student-recipe-best-bolognese-sauce/

500 g beef mince

1 glass red wine, optional

1 x quantity tomato sauce

Few dashes of Worcestershire sauce

2 large carrots, ends removed, coarsely grated

1 beef stock cube

Cooked pasta, to serve

Cheddar or Parmesan cheese, grated, to serve

Instructions

1. Heat one glug of oil in a large saucepan over high heat and fry the mushrooms, stirring occasionally, until soft and any liquid in the saucepan has evaporated—about five minutes. Empty the mushrooms into a bowl. Add another glug of oil to the saucepan, then add the mince. Stir to break it down and continue cooking until it's nicely browned.
2. Stir in the wine, if using. Bring to a boil, then turn down heat to medium, and simmer until most of the liquid has evaporated.
3. Add the tomato sauce, Worcestershire sauce, carrots, and cooked mushrooms. Crumble in the stock cube. Bring to a boil, then cover with a lid and simmer for forty-five minutes, stirring occasionally.
4. Serve with cooked pasta, topped with grated cheese.

Note: For nonmeat eaters, use veggie mince and stock, and leave out the Worcestershire sauce.

Dinner

Turmeric Chicken with Rice[4]

Ingredients (2 servings)

8 oz. (226 g) skinless and boneless chicken meat, breast or thigh, cut into strips

1 teaspoon turmeric powder

2 teaspoons oyster sauce

2 tablespoons oil

1/2 onion, sliced

1 red chili, deseeded and cut into thick strips

2 oz. (56 g) French bean, cut into two-inch strips

3 tablespoons water

1/2 teaspoon sugar

salt to taste

Instructions

---

4 https://rasamalaysia.com/turmeric-chicken/

1. Marinate the chicken with the turmeric powder and oyster sauce for fifteen minutes.
2. Heat up a wok and add the oil. Stir-fry the onion until aromatic, then add the chicken and do a few quick stirs.
3. Add the red chili, French beans, and stir well with the ingredients in the wok.
4. Add the water into the wok and continue to cook the chicken.
5. Add the sugar and salt (to taste), and continue stirring until the chicken is cooked through. Dish out and serve immediately with steamed rice.

Note: To make the meal prep for six days, triple the amount of ingredients. If you don't like it spicy, cut out the red chili. This recipe goes with rice or noodles.

2. Fitness and stress management

Be active

- Use the stairs instead of the elevator.

- Get at least thirty minutes of activity every day. If the idea of sweating at the gym for hours doesn't sound appealing to you, then head outside for a walk or jog.
- Join a dance or aerobics class on campus. Play indoor sports. Most important is to get yourself moving.

Relax

- Keep yourself organized to eliminate unnecessary and preventable stress.
- Turn off the TV and listen to music.
- Make time every day, even if it's just fifteen minutes, for relaxation and reflection.
- Take a nap.
- Allow at least thirty minutes of quiet relaxing activity before bed at night, such as reading a motivational book.
- Resist the temptation to use sleeping pills, when under the stress of writing papers, studying, and exam revision. Meditate instead.
- Sleep is not a waste of time. It's as important and necessary as nutrition and exercise.

Exercise at least three times a week. Exercise is good for your body and brain. Various studies have shown that exercise improves your memory; improves your brain function; reduces the occurrence of depression; helps to prevent diseases like diabetes, cancer, and osteoporosis; enhances your sleep quality; reduces stress; improves your mood; and increases your energy. Exercises such as dancing, yoga, and any cardio workouts can be done indoors through YouTube channels, if you find it inconvenient to join the physical classes.

Sleep at least eight hours a night. Not every student consistently gets eight hours of sleep a night. As a student, sleep often seems more like a luxury than a necessity. Research shows that if you get enough sleep, you'll be more focused, you'll learn faster, and your memory will improve. You'll also be able to deal with stress more effectively. So sleep at least eight hours a night. This way, your study sessions will be more productive, and you won't need to spend as much time hitting the books.

3. Social health

Get involved and meet people in a positive environment. Social health involves one's ability to form satisfying interpersonal relationships with others. It also relates to the ability to adapt comfortably to different social situations and act appropriately in a variety of settings. Often the adjustment to college can be difficult, especially when students are leaving the support from their parents they received for a lifetime. Joining a religious organization, volunteering at the orphanage, or helping in some other form of charity can give pleasure to many people.

When I was in London, I worked as a part-time interpreter and translator while studying full-time, and I enjoyed meeting the Chinese people who couldn't speak or write English and helped them translate the language. I was also a mentor to an autistic university student while studying my master's, and I helped her take notes in class, sat with her in the exam room, and assisted during her excursion for her architectural course. As a social worker, I used to teach immigrants English for communication to help them survive their day-to-day activities at the bank, market, and business. In the summer, I also volunteered to teach refugees and their children English, which lifted my spirits.

I believe that a healthy social life can enhance the immune system's ability to fight off infectious diseases. The most important thing to remember is to find something you are interested in and enjoy yourself while doing it. In a study, Robert Waldinger emphasizes the dangers of social isolation, stating that "loneliness kills" and it's as powerful as smoking or alcoholism. Thus, surrounding yourself with a positive social network increases your self-esteem. Social wellness enables you to create boundaries that encourage communication, trust, and conflict management. Having good social wellness is critical to building emotional resilience.

Living in a new norm of the COVID-19 pandemic, it is vital for everyone, especially students, to learn how to cope with their daily routine and study. Visit the Student Health Services in your institution to find out more information on maintaining a healthy lifestyle, diet, and any sports club that you can participate in. If you are in a lockdown situation, then make a new schedule and adapt to a new routine to keep your health, studies, and life going. Remember, when the going gets tough, the tough get going!

Stay healthy. Stay safe.

CHAPTER 12

WHAT IS COLLEGE DEPRESSION

If you had not suffered as you have, there would be no depth to you as a human being, no humility, no compassion.
—Eckhart Tolle

Did you know that one in four college students was diagnosed with a mental health disorder in the last year?

We all encounter the stresses of daily life, and college students in particular struggle with the adjustment to busy schedules and deadlines demanded from overwhelming courses and exams. The continuous pressure to achieve quickly during our early years of adulthood leads to college student stress, anxiety, and mental health challenges.

The first time we leave home and start preparing for adult life, college presents intense pressure to achieve high grades and shape successful careers. Students tend to push themselves to the limit both in their academic performance and their recreational outlets. When I was studying at the local college after being rejected for teacher's training, I was working full-time to support myself financially. I used to have various jobs such as teaching, banking, marketing, and so on, as I didn't stay in one job for long. I made little money, not enough to have my daily lunch at work.

At one point, a question crossed my mind—What am I going to do? "My brain is average, I'm not a top student, I don't have money for higher education, I don't like the job I do, I can't support my parents, I don't have the confidence. But I do know what I have. I have big dreams. I have an ambition. I know what I want. I want to be a graduate! I see other people have a degree. I believe I can have it too. I pray for that someday." That someday arrived. My dream came true. I am a graduate. That doesn't mean life is easy when you are a student. Your stress doesn't just come from your scores in study, but also from your personal life challenges. Suffering must come first before you achieve anything in life. Your bitterness now will soon turn to sweetness.

Many college students ignore signs of stress and, as a result, experience a range of physical, emotional, and behavioral symptoms. Increased heart rate or blood pressure, headaches, or fatigue, for example, commonly strains our physical states. The "psychological perception of pressure," on the other hand, influences our emotional reactions to unexpected situations.

College depression: What parents and teachers need to know

College depression has become a common problem in recent years. It is crucial for parents to know and understand why the transition to college makes young adults vulnerable to depression and how to deal with it.

The emotional transition from high school to college can be challenging. More freshmen and even mature students are struggling with depression than in the past. Learn how to spot if your child or a student is having trouble dealing with this new stage of life and how you can help.

What is college depression?

College depression is not a specific diagnosis. It is depression that happens during college mostly due to anxiety from the new routine, being independent, disoriented, heavy assignments, working with others, peer pressure, parents' expectation, unsupportive teachers, money issues, relationships, and exam stress.

Depression is a mood disorder that causes sadness and loss of interest for at least two weeks or longer. It is not just a bout of the blues or a sign of weakness, and you cannot just simply "snap out" of depression. I had depression while studying for my doctorate, and I was referred to the psychiatrist by my GP. There were a number of perspectives that I faced as a challenge—family, money, relationship, work, and study. I was prescribed antidepressant and sleeping pills. Those medications made me more sick than the depression itself. I needed to get the repeat prescription every three months, and this treatment would take a year with a clinical review once a month. I was tired and confused every day.

My depression had affected my research study, so I deferred for a year to focus on healing myself. I stopped everything altogether, from not taking the pills to not seeing the psychiatrist because I didn't want to believe I was at this stage being a mentally ill scholar. Although I was so lost, deep inside me somewhere, I felt I was much stronger.

It's hard to express how depression really is. It's kind of like sadness, but it's emotional, and I could burst into tears out of nowhere, crying for no reason and feeling so vulnerable, helpless, hopeless, and meaningless. It's like self-pity, self-doubt, worries, fear, and feeling unloved. I hated to have people around me. It's suicidal. In my mind, I thought life could be better and it couldn't just end without fulfillment. Suddenly, while weeping in the dark, some images appeared. I saw my young daughter, my late husband, my mom, my dad, my brothers and sisters, who were having so much hope for me. I could see their smiles, and I felt sorry for myself. My daughter lost her father when she was only eight months old, and she couldn't lose me at age six. I wanted to live on. So I decided to go for a long meditation retreat to bring my soul and senses back. I practiced Buddhism. I have learned the Buddhist philosophy for more than ten years. Eventually, Buddhism has made me a stronger person, and I became a better Christian all my life. I'm grateful for what I have accomplished.

Why are college students vulnerable to depression?

College students face challenges, pressures, and anxieties that can cause them to feel overwhelmed. They might feel homesick. Often for the first time in their lives, they are living on their own without any limits on their sleep schedules, the foods they choose to eat, and how much time they spend on activities such as video games or social media.

They are adapting to new schedules and workloads, adjusting to life with coursemates, and figuring out how to belong. Money and intimate relationships also can serve as major sources of stress. Dealing with these changes during the transition from adolescence to adulthood can trigger or unmask depression during college in some young adults. Furthermore, when students do not get the exam results they want, worrying that they may disappoint their parents and teachers, feeling too embarrassed to face their friends, thinking that they are of no use to the society and hopeless for the future, their suicidal thoughts set in and therefore attempt to end their lives.

How to recognize college depression

College students occasionally feel sad or anxious. These emotions usually pass within a few days. However, depression affects how a person feels, thinks, and behaves and can lead to a variety of emotional and physical problems.

Signs and symptoms that a student might be experiencing depression during college include the following:

- Feelings of sadness, tearfulness, emptiness, or hopelessness
- Irritability, frustration, and even angry outbursts—out of proportion to the situation
- Loss of interest or pleasure in most or all normal activities, such as hobbies or sports
- Sleep disturbances, including insomnia or sleeping too much
- Tiredness and lack of energy; even small tasks take extra effort
- Changes in appetite—often reduced appetite and weight loss, but increased cravings for food and weight gain in some people
- Negative changes in academic performance
- Unexplained physical problems, such as back pain or headaches
- Anxiety, agitation, or restlessness
- Feelings of worthlessness or guilt, fixating on past failures, or blaming yourself for things that are not your responsibility
- Trouble thinking, concentrating, making decisions, and remembering things
- Frequent or recurrent thoughts of death, suicidal thoughts, suicide attempts, or suicide

What to do if you think you or your friend is experiencing college depression

Signs and symptoms of depression might be harder to notice if the student is not living at home. Thus, faculty members or lecturers will need to step in and help by arranging the student to see a counselor to diagnose the problem. Some college students also might have difficulty seeking help for depression out of embarrassment or fear of not fitting in. Many college students do not get treatment for depression although the college provides counseling facilities.

If you think a student might be dealing with depression, talk to him or her about the problem and listen. Encourage them to share his or her feelings with you or someone else trusted, such as a counselor or a doctor, and to book an appointment as soon as possible.

If you suspect that you may be depressed and your health is at risk or cannot cope with your study and day-to-day routine, seek help from the college counselor or see a medical doctor for advice. Most colleges offer mental health services, though they may be limited. Colleges may not offer long-term help but may be able to provide information on local doctors and therapists who can help. However, you may try to talk to your closest friend or a sibling to let them help you. If nothing else helps, I suggest you read a self-help book, *You Can Heal Your Life* by Louise Hay, or Google search for her inspirational videos.

How to cope with depression in college

In addition to seeking treatment, there are five easy ways to help you destress and feel better:

1. **Take it one step at a time**

Avoid doing too many things at once. Instead, break up large tasks into small ones. Try different time-management methods to suit you. Relax.

2. **Keep a healthy lifestyle**

Do daily exercises, eat well, spend time in nature, get enough sleep, pray, and avoid alcohol, drugs, and tobacco. Using alcohol and drugs is a poor way to cope with stress and may contribute to the development of depression. Go for a massage or spa once in a while to chill out. Have a new daily routine.

3. **Seek support**

Spend time with supportive family members and friends or seek out student support groups. Join online courses on self-healing, learn a new skill, or attend a life-changing webinar from a well-known coach. Seek spiritual help.

4. **Have fun**

Try to have fun with a new hobby. Travel to find enjoyment. College clubs and activities can be a great place to make friends and try something new. Read inspirational quotes or a good book on personal development. Try yoga or dance. Go for a movie. Volunteer for charity. Join a marathon.

5. **Listen to positive affirmation**

Get a collection of CDs, podcasts, audiobooks, or YouTube videos on positive affirmation, meditation, and inspirational speech to boost positive thinking and happiness. Practice mindfulness exercises.

How can parents and teachers help prevent college depression?

There's no surefire way to prevent depression during college. However, helping the student become accustomed to his or her college campus before the start of the new semester might prevent the student from feeling overwhelmed by the transition. Pay a visit to the campus and talk to other students, parents, counselors, or faculty about what to expect and where to turn for support. However, students can prevent depression by doing the five easy ways above to start off as a routine to form a new habit so that they can cope with stress before it turns into serious depression.

Besides, Dr. Marcia Morris, a college mental health psychiatrist and an associate professor of psychiatry at the University of Florida, suggested to parents the five *T*s: tell, test, teach, talk, and take action:

- *Tell* your child they can come to you with any problem
- *Test* their academic health by checking their end-of-semester grades
- *Teach* them how to recognize depression and anxiety
- *Talk* with them more often or visit if they are in distress
- *Take* action if your student is experiencing high-risk mental health concerns

Factors that cause students anxiety at college

- Studying a new language
- Subject difficulty
- Difficulty in exams
- Financial pressure
- Culture shock
- Family responsibilities
- Illness
- Employment
- Discrimination
- Disabilities
- Peer pressure
- Assignment overload
- Boy-girl relationships

Students at higher education institutions face many kinds of challenges that negatively affect their psychological feelings, causing them anxiety. Its effects vary among students in how to deal with it, overcome its symptoms, and find solutions.

Depression might get worse if it is not treated. Untreated depression can lead to other mental and physical health issues or problems in college and other areas of life. Feelings of depression can get in the way of a student's academic success. They can also increase the likelihood of high-risk behaviors, such as binge drinking, substance abuse, unsafe sex, and risk of suicide. It is important for parents, teachers, and students to read this chapter and understand the fundamental cause of college depression and what to do with it. In addition, parents can read and learn more about helping your child to survive in college.[5]

How to prevent attempting suicide[6]

If you feel suicidal, give yourself the opportunity to express your own feelings, speak aloud so that you can provide relief from loneliness and pent-up negative feelings; doing so may prevent a suicide attempt. I know you don't want to die, and nobody really wants to kill themselves. Before anything happens, speak to somebody, listen to an audiobook by Louise Hay, or watch an inspirational video on YouTube that can help you change your mind. When you overcome your challenges and frustrated situations, you will have a bright future to look forward to and leave all the suicidal thoughts behind. While searching for more insights into writing this book, I found this inspiring message:

> *When I was 18, I had no direction in my life. I was depressed, suicidal and addicted to drugs. I didn't think my life could get any worse, but then I lost my mother and father in a freak car accident. That was the final straw for me, I had no one else in my life, no reason to live. I threw my body off a bridge in an attempt to kill myself, but as soon as I began to fall, I immediately regretted it. Suddenly, I saw all of the things I wanted to achieve in life flash before my eyes. Marrying a beautiful girl, starting a family with her and becoming a doctor.*

---

5 M. Morris, *The Campus Cure: A Parent's Guide to Mental Health and Wellness for College Students* (Rowman & Littlefield, 2018).
6 https://www.helpguide.org/articles/suicide-prevention/suicide-prevention.htm

As these things vividly flashed before me, I could hear a voice that I could only describe as ethereal. It was at that moment that the Lord decided to save me! I miraculously survived the fall, which baffled every medical professional that checked on me. I knew that GOD had spared me because he had great plans for me, and that gave me the will to carry on. That was 10 years ago. I am now a qualified medical professional, and tomorrow I will be proposing to my girlfriend of 4 years. Wish me luck my fellow brothers and sisters in Christ! God bless you all. (Anonymous)

You have two choices: leave or live. Choosing to die will not solve your problems. It shows how immature you are. You will only hurt your loved ones when they lose you forever. If anyone has done something bad to you, and you hate them to bits, or you may hate yourself when you didn't get what you expect or what others expect of you, it's not your fault. Look at yourself in the mirror and say this twenty times now: "I am sorry. Please forgive me. Thank you. I love you."

You are speaking to your inner child. Do this first thing you wake up for the next twenty-one days. You will love yourself more and find your strength. Remember, every human being is bound to leave the world with a legacy. What have you contributed to your life?

Sending my love to you. You are always great!

CHAPTER 13

WHERE TO GET MORE HELP

> It's not the lack of resources that causes failure; it's
> the lack of resourcefulness that causes failure.
> —Tony Robbins

During college, the biggest worries students face should be studying for their next exam, and the big party they'll throw when it's finished. However, a lack of funds may force highly motivated and successful students to take a semester off or even drop out of their college.

For students who are struggling financially, figuring out how to pay for tuition, rent, books, food, and all the other expenses of college life can take a serious toll, with the stress affecting their studies. Some students can turn to parents or other relatives for assistance. Others may need to navigate their cash flow challenges themselves. But even if you fall into the latter group, you're not alone. Money is usually the number one concern for students pursuing higher education. Apart from tuition fees, you also need a living allowance and pocket money. Therefore, it is wise to plan and prepare yourself financially before you apply to study in college or university, and that is as soon as you finish your high school final exams. If you can't find any sponsors for your study, take a break and work for at least a couple of years or until you raise enough money to fund your first semester study.

Financial help for college students is available through on- and off-campus organizations and resource centers that provide assistance in various forms. For instance, a scholarship from the college or study loan from the government may be obtainable to help you with your tuition fees and living expenses. If all don't work, you have to get yourself a part-time job or sell something online. Join online affiliate marketing, such as Clickbank and Amazon. Do this only if you're already started your semester well but need money to support your daily or other expenses.

There are resources available everywhere. and students have to be resourceful because it is the lack of resourcefulness that causes people to fail. Resourcefulness means having the ability to find quick and clever ways to overcome difficulties. You are never short of resources. The dream is not the problem—it's the dreamer, and that's *you!*

Here's a list of exceptional resources for college students that you can turn to, or share with a friend, when personal goals and finances become a concern.

A Vision for Success

When you know better, you do better. As a tertiary student, you need to have a *vision* in order to be successful. Your vision should be seeing yourself as a graduate! This is a short-term goal. For long-term goals, you will plan what you want after you graduate, and this could be your career, your dream life-partner, financial independence, children, vacation, a business, a PhD, and so on. The process of getting your vision visible may be difficult, but not impossible. I believe that new college students can be trained and coached in order to improve and succeed in their studies. Be resourceful. Thus, whether you are studying foundation or in your first year of higher education, where you may face challenges in your study, I suggest that you check out the facility and what is available in your institution for a start. You may also use Google to search the available articles on study skills; watch motivational videos that help you succeed; join a student group on social media; talk to your college advisor; or discuss with people you can trust. If you're unwell or stressed, see a medical doctor to find out the cause.

Schools don't teach personal skills like how to study or how to manage money and stress. I hope the future school curriculum will include these important and essential components for children to grow before they enter college. The study skills I show you in this book are how I applied and successfully completed my formal academic education along the way from a college certificate up to a doctorate degree. I was only an average student, and I made myself above average. I am a self-made graduate. I made changes and amendments along the way for over fifteen years since entering college up to obtaining a PhD, not from kindergarten, primary, or secondary school, as no teacher taught me the skills to excel in school.

I learned study skills at the university. I did trial and error. The skills not only worked for me, but also for my students, who benefited from the plan and guidance I taught them. It was a success for me and my students, and I am sharing the formula with you in this book.

There are things you need to know how to prevent before it gets to you as it will affect your studies, and not knowing it sooner may slow down your progress in your overall life as a student. I have covered most of the necessary elements for you to survive in college in the previous chapters. Nevertheless, here's what you can do in order to enhance your dreams and goals.

Make a Vision Board

A vision board is a collage of images and words representing a person's wishes or goals, intended to serve as inspiration or motivation. It is created to help visualize and focus on one or more specific aspirations you want in your life. When I was studying in London many years ago, I never heard of vision boards. I wrote my goals in my little red diary. I drew a triangle and put my academic goals by each level from the lowest up to a PhD at the tip of the triangle. That was my dream, my long-term goals, and I achieved all of them. It was in recent years that I encountered vision boards from YouTube, and I followed Terri Saville's podcasts on making a vision board.

Apart from my own achievement in reaching my goals one after another in the last three years, since I created a vision board in 2017, I also taught my daughter, Jade, to make herself a vision board while studying in high school. We went to the local DIY shop and got the corkboard, alphabet stickers, and pushpins. Jade has had eczema since she was a few months old, and one of her goals was to have clear and healthy skin. She printed some nice color pictures of beautiful girls with smooth and lovely skin, and healthy food alongside. She made the vision board sometime in 2018. In the following year, Jade's eczema was cleared and healed, and today she has smooth and healthy skin. When you have a vision, stop worrying about the process and how your goals will come true. It matters what you do and who will come into your life that will make your dreams come true. It could be a prayer answered. Somebody may appear as a godsend.

What is your big dream? What are your ultimate goals? Why are they important to you? When do you want to achieve them? Are you ready for this? Start NOW!

1. **Write down your goals**

Begin with the basic things that you desire. Which university would you like to attend? What degree would you like to graduate with? Where would you like to travel? What would you like to own? How much money would you like to save by this December? Where would you like to work? Who would you like to meet? What is your ideal body weight?

Just get started with your basic desires. Write your fifty goals in your journal or a notebook. For example, your list may start as follows to be specific:

- I want to get a scholarship fully paid for my degree course.
- I want to be a first class honors graduate.
- I want to travel to the seven wonders of the world.
- I want to meet Jeff Bezos.
- I want to attend Harvard University.
- I want to earn US$20,000 a month.
- I want to own a house on the hill.
- I want to publish a best seller book.

Start writing whatever comes to your mind. Anything that comes to your mind when you're writing and whatever pops into your head, you are putting a demand on yourself to dream. You may list fun and adventurous things such as climbing the highest mountain in Southeast Asia, skydiving, meeting someone famous, sailing alone, and so on. The more you write, the more you will discover your true ambitions. Don't ask yourself how to get what you desire. Just dream the things you want in your life. Believe in your dreams. Use your imagination. Imagine it is five or ten years from now and you are living the life of your dreams. What does it look like? What type of degree do you receive? Where do you live? Where do you work? How much money can you give to charity? What do you do for fun? What do you drive? Just dream. Imagine. Visualize. Where do you vacation? Close your eyes and imagine you're walking on the sandy beach in Hawaii feeling relaxed and joyful with your loved ones.

2. **Create your vision board**

Designing a vision board is like framing your future before it ever happens. It is indeed a fun exercise my daughter and I enjoy. Create the vision board by referring to your list of top ten goals. Browse online to print or look through magazines to cut the pictures you want that represent your goals. Type and print out the wordings you want to place next to the pictures. Use present tense for the words. The materials you need to make a vision board are one medium-size corkboard, pushpins, and alphabet or number stickers. Make sure the size of every picture and the wording fits in your corkboard. Below is an example on how to transfer your important goals to a vision board.

Goal #1: Save $5,000

Print out a picture of cash, or use a real banknote. Clearly pin these wordings below or next to the photo or banknote: *Save $5,000 by 31st December 20__*.

Goal #2: Receive an Honors Degree

Get a graduation picture showing a person holding a scroll. Write near to the picture, "Receive a 1st Class Honors Degree by 1 February 20__," and include the name of your institution. You may replace the face in the picture with yours if you like, and that makes it more interestingly real.

Goal #3: Vacation in Hawaii

Cut out pictures of Hawaii from travel brochures, the resort you desire to stay, and the specific itinerary of places you want to visit. Find out the cost to achieve this goal, such as flight, hotel, excursions, meals, and so on. Write the vision and make it plain, "Vacation in Hawaii by 15th June 20__, $6,582," next to the pictures.

Keep your vision board as neat as possible, and use numbers next to each goal. Arrange your pictures and your goals in the order that appeals to you. You may use two corkboards each for study goals, short-term; and personal goals, long-term. Once your vision board is completed, hang it on the wall or keep it in front of you on your study desk so that you can view your goals every day. Remember to keep your dreams in front of you, as the saying goes, out of sight, out of mind.

3. **Build your faith**

While waiting for your dreams to manifest, build your faith. The first habit to adapt into your new routine is listening to motivational and positive teachings. If you have a religion, pray for intelligence and opportunities, and have 100 percent faith that you will receive. You need faith to achieve your dreams. Through faith, all my dreams came true no matter how long I waited. I remember I prayed so hard that I would study overseas to get a degree and be a graduate. That was my priority, and that was what I wanted so badly. I always believed I could achieve everything I planned and visualized. I had faith. A year later, my opportunity appeared. You can reach any one goal you set out in your vision board for as fast as three months, though some goals may take longer to achieve. No matter how long it takes, don't shrink your dreams, enlarge your faith instead. Less talk. More action.

Prayers

People tend to remember their religious teachers or elders and seek some blessings for guidance and protection when they are in trouble. Before that, they didn't think it's necessary to pray or live a spiritual life. Regrettably I did just that. I prayed hard for my vision to study overseas until my prayers were answered. When I got the opportunity to study in England, I was so desperate to achieve what I planned to do. I worked really hard, and I had three part-time jobs and studied full-time for a degree. I forgot how to pray. I graduated, and here I was in my next hurdle for a master's degree. Again, I prayed for my vision to get a scholarship, and I got it.

All this while I didn't have the time to go to church, and I prayed only when I was in need of help. I always believe that I'm so blessed and God loves me dearly that He gave me a gift—my daughter, and He took my husband away to be with Him. But then I was confused and lost direction. I questioned myself, Who am I? What am I doing in this world? Why me? God wanted to redirect my life. He said, "Seek and you shall find." So I learned and practiced the Buddhist way of life for more than ten years, and I gained so much wisdom that I didn't even realize how much I had changed to be mindful until I returned to Christianity. I'm a better Christian today.

Now I understand that having faith is an essence in life, and it guides us to the right direction when we are in trouble. Hence, the trouble itself can be part of God's plan. Nothing in this world is permanent, including one's suffering. We say, "This too shall pass," as mentioned in the Scriptures. Furthermore, "the main purpose of a religion is to help us to follow certain noble principles to avoid many self-made problems by training our mind before they confront us and cause misery" (K Sri Dhammananda 2004).

Dream as big as you can and declare what you believe. Listen to the positive words coming out of your mouth. Pray to God.

Believe in the vibration of the universe. If you're not going to speak faith, don't speak at all. Words are powerful. Words can be a salvation, and it can be a damnation. So talk like you already have what you're praying for. I have prayed as a Christian, and I also prayed as a Buddhist. Both in different occasions and contexts. Try listening to inspirational speeches by religious leaders or motivational preachers on YouTube. Make it a routine and habit. I still watch these inspirational, motivational, and affirmation videos on YouTube every morning.

Meditation

The aim of meditation isn't about becoming a different person, a new person, or even a better person. You're not trying to turn off your thoughts or feelings but learning to observe them without judgment. Through meditation, you can reduce stress, increase calmness and clarity, and promote happiness. It is also a practice where one uses a technique, such as mindfulness, to train attention and awareness. Mindfulness is the ability to be present, to rest in the here and now, fully engaged with whatever we're doing in the moment. You acknowledge the present moment and are aware of your breathing.

Are you worried? Do you have many what-if thoughts? If so, you are projecting an imaginary future situation and creating fear. There is no medication that can help with your thoughts and mind—only meditation. When you believe in your dreams and goals, you imagine and visualize the good outcome that you desire in the future without worry or fear. However, it is not right when you doubt what you imagine and visualize, or you're worried about the process and how it would happen. Such thoughts create anxiety, stress, fear, and disappointment, and that will result in depression.

Meditation has helped me overcome my depression while I was studying my doctorate. That year was a year of disaster for me. Everything seemed to happen at the same time. I fell from the stairs at the train station and injured my knee badly and was off work for six months; I was cheated by someone whom I trusted, betrayed by my colleagues, and experiencing complications in my health. My daughter was only six, and I simply couldn't cope with my family. I got into depression. I was prescribed antidepressant and sleeping pills by the psychiatrist. I didn't have much of this kind of stress when I was studying in England. My kind of stress then was due to financial constraints, and my solution to lacking money was to work, work, and work. I was busy working and attending lectures and doing my assignments. My break time was the summer holiday, but then I was working full-time throughout the summer. I got through my undergraduate and postgraduate studies without being depressed.

Mindfulness, an important life skill that is not taught in school. The easiest formula for us to follow and practice is being mindful and living in the present. Mindfulness practices can help us to increase our ability to regulate emotions, decrease stress, anxiety, and depression. It can also help us to focus our attention as well as to observe our thoughts and feelings without judgment. Some motivational gurus such as Eckhart Tolle and Louise Hay teach us this: what you think and what you believe will come true for you. That's what the law of thinking is. Your thoughts create your life. I have learned this philosophy in Buddhism. From growing up a Catholic and not knowing how to understand Scripture to acquiring the

Buddhist teachings and becoming a better Christian. Thus, I learned from Scripture that our thoughts are powerful. They can harm us or do us good. The Bible says, "For as he thinks within himself, so is he" (Proverbs 23:7).

I learned meditation when I was practicing Buddhism in Malaysia, and there are different types of meditation techniques that I encountered and experienced. It's a great journey God has put me into—to rid misery and change my life for good. I am still the same person, but the difference is the way I think, see, and approach anything that has changed. For instance, I remain calm when criticism strikes and when things happen beyond my control. You can try the breathing meditation technique as a beginner. Search on YouTube to learn the different types of meditation, find and practice the one that most suits your style and condition.

Support Services and Resources

It is not unusual for even the best high school students to find themselves struggling in college. Most colleges and universities provide academic support programs to help students succeed. You should seek assistance as soon as you receive poor grades or feel that you are falling behind. If all the other students seem to know what they are doing and you are still confused by the third or fourth lecture, it is time to take action. Speak to your lecturer or the college counselor if it is related to your grades. If they are not helpful, you can discuss with your parents, siblings, coursemates, or close friends. Another option is to read other self-help books, if this book doesn't help your current situation. In the end, it is the truly smart students who seek help!

When you feel lonely, pick up a new hobby and get to know like-minded people who enjoy doing the same activities. Start an online business according to your passion. Join an interest club or participate in community activities such as charity or volunteering to help in orphanage homes. Share your experiences with people you meet; this may be the start of new and fulfilling friendships. When you are brokenhearted, receive poor grades, fail in your exams, or can't make it to the next semester, it's not the end of the world. When there's a problem, there's a solution. If a problem has no solution, then why bother solving it? Why worry? There are plenty of resources out there to solve any problems and personal challenges. You know how to use social media and ask Google for anything. Be resourceful.

Remember, always be thankful and show gratitude with what you have and who you're with. Good or bad. Say thank-you to God or the universe every day and any time of the day, even though you have not received what you're aiming for or not being treated how you hoped for. Good things will come to those who show their gratitude even before they see and receive them.

I wish you the best in your study and life!

INSPIRATIONAL SUCCESS STORIES

> The will to win, the desire to succeed, the urge to reach your full potential . . . these are the keys that will unlock the door to personal excellence.
> —Confucius

Case Study 1

As a schoolteacher of almost three decades, and at age forty-two, I felt that I needed to equip myself with the latest techniques and methods of teaching, especially in technology. So I decided to upgrade my status by pursuing a degree. I enrolled at the International Islamic University Malaysia to study for a bachelor of education. Being the most senior in class, I was determined to do well as higher education would help me broaden my horizons and also increase my income in the future.

As a mature student, maintaining the level of motivation to study can be tricky as I had to endure challenges that I was not sure if I could handle. Since I was studying full-time, I had to stop teaching in school, and it was a challenge to face commitments like paying bills and settling loans. The cost of the degree was daunting too. Another challenge that I faced was uncertainty as I was not sure if I could go through the whole program.

I spent so much time studying, especially preparing for assignments and examinations. I was overwhelmed balancing multiple classes and personal life commitments. However, with a positive mindset, I overcame all my problems by prioritizing and planning my coursework properly.

Never give up without a struggle even if you have failed in the semester. Obviously, you need to reassess yourself and try to find solutions to your problem. If you look at failures as learning experiences, then those very failures become your motivator and eventually lead you toward success. You need to practice and develop your own study skills. Besides, the skill of managing your time is important to ensure you accomplish the specific tasks assigned to you on time.

If you are about to enter college and university, my advice is, always have a positive mindset and empower yourself to have a happier and more successful life. It was through my empowered mindset that I obtained first class honors and was in the dean's list of excellent academic achievement. I think learning study skills not only improves your performance but also your ability to learn in general, which benefits you for the rest of your life.

Lai Yong Yin
STEM Ambassador Malaysia

Case Study 2

I decided to study for a degree in my thirties because I wanted to gain more knowledge and improve my employability prospect. I was working in a legal firm, so I chose to study Law (LLB) from the University of London external program. I studied on a part-time basis, both by distance learning and attending evening and weekend classes at a private college. It was tough studying part-time as I had to work full-time from Monday to Friday.

I was struggling during my first semester preparing for my first-year exam, which was held midyear. I had four subjects to prepare for the exam each year. I was given assignments when I attended classes in college; however, all assignments did not carry any marks toward any of the actual examinations set by the university as the degree course is based on 100 percent closed-book examinations. I was extremely busy preparing for the examinations and quite stressed because I had to juggle a full-time job and my studies. However, I was able to manage my stress level and still enjoyed my studies amid the hectic and tight schedule as this was what I had always wanted to study since I was in my early twenties.

As a mature student, firstly, I had to fund my own studies, and that was only possible when I was in full-time employment. I had to use whatever savings and income that I had to pay for my course fees, classes, and examinations, as well as other expenses. Secondly, due to time constraints as a result of working full-time and studying part-time, I had to have proper time management and self-discipline.

When you enter college or university, choose the course that you are most interested in studying. Research thoroughly before making your final decision to enroll for the course to be sure this is what you want to study. Obtain the necessary pre-degree qualifications or prerequisites required by the college or university for the course you are interested in studying. Make sure the course and the college or university you have chosen to study are recognized internationally, including in your home country.

My advice to students is not to give up on your study even if you fail your semester. Find ways and means to improve your study skills and continue your studies until you reach the finish line. Students need to learn study skills, which is the prerequisite of success in studying any course. Good study skills and good time management are key. And most importantly, cultivate self-discipline as it will lead you to be successful in anything that you wish to achieve.

Patrick Hiew
Human Resource Manager

Case Study 3

I started my higher education at seventeen and spent four years before graduating. I studied full-time. It was a mix of attending classes as well as practical hands-on sessions. It was easy for the first year, and it became increasingly hard later because the course was a pioneer joint course at the Polytechnic in Singapore. I chose engineering and IT, but I didn't get the right information, so I studied a bunch of stuff that I had absolutely no interest in and was very weak at.

As someone who is pretty introverted, I had to learn to socialize with my peers, and that was difficult. I always preferred spending time by myself, but as the course wasn't something I was interested in by year 2 (the first year were subjects I was interested in, and I aced them), the following years were absolute torture to get through.

For students who are about to enter college and university, I suggest you make lots of friends; you really don't know where further down the road you might meet those people again. Some of the people you meet might be weak in their studies, but when they get out into real life, they might succeed really well. Maintain the relationships you've built because it's the only time when you can really get to know people without being judged on how successful you are in life. Even if you're struggling with your studies, just by working hard together with your peers, you just might get a friend for life.

If you fail the semester, don't drop out of college. Do your best and complete it. I was super tempted to fail it all and completely drop out of my studies and get to work. However, I knew that it was a mindset thing. If I drop out just because it was tough, in the working world, you can't just drop out of something and expect things to go on as per normal. If life decides to give you challenges at this point in time, I assure you tons of other people have also successfully graduated. Some did it easily, some had to struggle, but they all still graduated.

I wish I knew how to study back then. All I did was to turn my textbooks into coloring books by highlighting pretty much everything. When you have your study skills locked in, those skills stick with you and evolve into other wondrous forms of education. Becoming a graduate is proof you're good at projects, work, and interpersonal relationships. Students should acquire communication and presentation skills. Knowing how to communicate and present yourself and your ideas well will give you a natural advantage in the future workplace.

Asher Aw
Online Coach

BIBLIOGRAPHY

Alkandari, N. Y. *Students Anxiety Experiences in Higher Education Institutions.* DOI: 10.5772/intechopen.92079.

Burns, T., and S. Sinfield. *Essential Study Skills: The Complete Guide to Success at University.* Sage Publications, 2012.

Cepeda, N. J., V. Edward, D. Rohrer, J. T. Wixted, and H. Pashler. *Spacing Effects in Learning: A Temporal Ridgeline of Optimal Retention.* 2008. doi.org/10.1111/j.1467-9280.2008.02209.

Cottrell, S. *The Study Skills Handbook.* Palgrave Macmillan, 2013.

Dhammananda, K. Sri. *You and Your Problems.* Kuala Lumpur: Buddhist Missionary Society Malaysia, 2004.

Dweck, C. "The Perils and Promises of Praise." *Educational Leadership* 65, no. 2 (October 2007): 34–39.

Hay, L. L. *You Can Heal Your Life.* Santa Monica, CA: Hay House, 1987.

Hibbs, B. J. and A. Rostain. *The Stressed Years of Their Lives: Helping Your Kid Survive and Thrive during Their College Years.* St. Martin's Press, 2019.

Martin, D. *How to Be a Successful Student.* Marin Trails Publishing, 1993.

Morris, M. *The Campus Cure: A Parent's Guide to Mental Health and Wellness for College Students.* Rowman & Littlefield, 2018.

Mueller, P. A., and D. M. Oppenheimer. *The Pen Is Mightier Than the Keyboard: Advantages of Longhand Over Laptop Note Taking.* Sage Publications, 2014.

Saville, T. *Dream It. Pin It. Live It: Make Vision Boards Work for You.* USA: Terri Saville Foy Ministry, 2015.

Willis, J. "Building a Bridge from Neuroscience to the Classroom." *Phi Delta Kappan* 89, no. 6 (2008): 424–427.

Yehuda, S. "Omega-6/Omega-3 Ratio and Brain-Related Functions." *World Review of Nutrition and Dietetics* 92 (2003): 37–56.

Website Sources

https://www.headspace.com/meditation-101/what-is-meditation

https://www.nytimes.com/guides/well/how-to-meditate

https://teens.lovetoknow.com/Characteristics_of_a_Good_Friend

https://www.moneyprodigy.com/personal-goals-examples-for-students/

https://www.fundi.co.za/fundiconnect/student-dropout-causes/

https://www.govst.edu/suicide-prevention/

https://www.rhodes.edu/admission-aid/admitted-students/health-forms/health-awareness/tips-maintaining-good-health

https://vulcanpost.com/548841/msian-entrepreneur-who-dropped-out-of-college/

https://www.govst.edu/stress-less/

https://www.statista.com/statistics/1126279/percentage-of-college-students-with-depression-us/

https://www.ncbi.nlm.nih.gov/pmc/articles/PMC3057910/

https://www.affordablecollegesonline.org/college-resource-center/college-student-depression/

https://www.bu.edu/articles/2021/depression-anxiety-loneliness-are-peaking-in-college-students/

https://www.bestcolleges.com/research/college-mental-health-impacts-from-covid-19/

https://www.voanews.com/archive/spielberg-fulfills-dream-graduates-college

https://www.insidehighered.com/advice/2020/10/28/advice-how-successfully-guide-students-group-work-online-opinion

https://thesmartlocal.com/malaysia/counselling-mental-health-services/

https://www.nami.org/Blogs/NAMI-Blog/December-2018/A-Parent-s-Guide-to-Mental-Health-for-College-Students

https://www.intechopen.com/books/anxiety-disorders-the-new-achievements/students-anxiety-experiences-in-higher-education-institutions

https://kappanonline.org/willis-bridge-neuroscience-classroom/

https://www.daniel-wong.com/2015/08/17/study-smart/

https://www.helpguide.org/articles/mental-disorders/narcissistic-personality-disorder.htm

https://www.healthline.com/nutrition/11-brain-foods

https://steverosephd.com/what-is-social-health/

https://www.medicalnewstoday.com/articles/263648#1

https://www.studyandexam.com/making-study-plan.html

https://www.thecompleteuniversityguide.co.uk/student-advice/after-you-start/how-to-revise-for-exams-top-tips

https://help.open.ac.uk/revising-with-others

https://www.pcmag.com/how-to/10-tips-for-managing-your-digital-notes

https://www.wjec.co.uk/articles/5-reasons-why-you-should-use-past-papers-in-your-revision/

ABOUT THE AUTHOR

Dream with your imagination of who you want to be. At the same time, feel the excitement as though your dream has come true.
—*Dr. Yolanda Hiew*

Dr. Yolanda Hiew (best known as Dr. Y) is the founder and CEO of Pro-Study Academy, which she started in 2021 as a way to share her personal lifelong learning experience and to make study easier for college students. Since then, Dr. Y has grown her *study formula* into one of the most popular websites in the world, with her online study skill course catered for her students before they pursued higher education. Due to her passion in education and lifelong learning, Dr. Y invested in MindAppz, an education and e-learning platform in 2016, as a franchisor and merchant where she published her two e-books that attracted more than seven thousand downloads. Her first e-book, *How to Overcome the Obstacles in Your Study*, became the best seller on MindAppz, which has more than one hundred thousand users since 2017, and her *Success Skills at Higher Education* is rated five stars.

In April 2020, after the lockdown in Malaysia, with Movement Control Order due to the COVID-19 pandemic, Dr. Y began to search for personal development courses and training to update her knowledge and social media skills. After attending several seminars and online courses, she found the Passion Purpose Profits (PPP) 5 Days Challenge, conducted by the Facebook Queen, Suria Mohd @ Suria Sparks at iSuccess Academy, a Singapore-based learning hub that focuses on personal development, entrepreneurship, positive parenting, exam techniques, and nutrition. After completing the PPP, Dr. Y was mentored by Suria Sparks to discover self-love for body and mind, and she learned new skills on social media marketing and branding. As part of her personal growth, Dr. Y was featured in the iSuccess Global Wall of Fame and later became the cofounder at iSuccess Academy Online School, where she has promoted and conducted training.

With over ten years of pursuing higher education, including her doctorate study, and twenty years as a lecturer, mentor, and coach, Dr. Y is still just as passionate about pushing her limits as a lifelong learner and teacher and sharing her secrets on surviving at college and study skills as she was when she began. While serving as a lecturer, she designed one of the bachelor's degree courses for English education and was approved by the Ministry of Education, Malaysia. Through her efforts, today, Pro-Study Academy is a world-class education center collaborating with MindAppz, a no. 1 Malaysia digital learning platform that is going global. Dr. Y still retains its start-up mentality, where she has taught thousands of tertiary students and personally coached over one hundred students since 2017 to make personal breakthroughs at work and at home. Apart from being an expert in study skills, Dr. Y is also an English specialist, and many of her students obtained straight As, and most of them have pursued their studies overseas. Dr. Y is a valued guest speaker and contributor to numerous reputable institutions in Malaysia and England. She has participated in an interview organized by MindAppz on *Hey Mom, Dad, Do I Really Need to Go to College?* via Facebook live in August 2020.

Dr. Y quickly made a name for herself, and the initial popularity of her shared "study formula and how to live your life as a student" was overwhelming because it addressed a common need that college and mature students had. This response made Dr. Y realize that creating an online course and writing an extensive book on study skills for tertiary students would help in her calling to help students ace in exams and become a high achiever in life. There was a new mission—to positively influence more and more students through this knowledge and expertise. Dr. Y quit her physical English classes and launched her first company and became an entrepreneur and coach dedicated to Pro-Study Academy, fully online, to fulfill this goal. As a determined learner and teacher, she has participated in various virtual conventions, international summits, master class workshops, and self-development courses and trainings. Nowadays, Dr. Y spends more time writing e-books and online courses and coaching her teenage daughter, preparing her for tertiary study and to be the next generation of productivity guru.

Brief overview of Dr. Yolanda Hiew's higher educational background:

- Subediting and design diploma, London School of Journalism, England
- ILEX certificate in vocational legal studies (level 2), Newham College of Further Education, England
- BA (Hons) linguistics and education and community studies, University of East London, England
- Teaching international English for business, London Guildhall University (now London Metropolitan University), England
- Master of arts in applied linguistics, Birkbeck, University of London
- Doctor of philosophy, Universiti Putra Malaysia
- Recipient of the Reeve Foundation Scholarship (merit-based), UK

Dr. Yolanda Hiew's teaching journey:

- Japanese International School, Malaysia
- Woodford Adult Education Centre, England
- University of East London, England
- Universiti Tunku Abdul Rahman, Malaysia
- University of Nottingham Malaysia Campus

- Universiti Putra Malaysia
- Cambridge English for Life, Malaysia
- Cambridge Language Centre, Malaysia
- Home and Online Tuition for English Conversation, IELTS, IGCSE, IB, UEC, SPM exams

Courses and workshops attended and completed, to list just a few:

- English for Business Communication
- Proofreader Plus
- Note-Taking for Lectures
- Disability and Dyslexia Awareness
- Introduction to Community Interpreting
- Personal Grooming and Image Building
- Cooperative Learning
- Critique the Rhetoric and Reality of ICT Integration in Learning and Teaching
- Fundamental Principles of Testing/Assessment
- The Theory and Practice of Learning and Teaching in Higher Education
- Research Methodology for Social Science: A Qualitative Approach
- Vipassana Meditation, Dhamma Malaya
- Social Media Marketing and Branding, iSuccess Academy, Singapore
- Paradigm Shift and Secrets to Successful Living, Proctor Gallagher Institute, USA
- Vision 101, Terri Savelle Ministry, USA
- Professional Counselling Diploma, UK

And so on and so forth. And she's continuously learning from legendary mentors—Jim Rohn, Dr. J. Demartini, Bob Proctor,

Les Brown, Jack Canfield, Brian Tracy, Tony Robbins, Dr. Joe Dispenza, Eckhart Tolle, Louise Hay, Terri Savelle, and many more.

If you have anything about learning, count me in! - Dr. Y

Photos Contribution Credit to

George Milton
Marko Klaric
Ivan Samkov
Jade Alexandra
Mikhail Nilov
Sarah Chai
Andrea Piacquadio
Pixabay
Pexels

Lightning Source UK Ltd.
Milton Keynes UK
UKHW011850140921
390594UK00001B/77